WHAT PEOPLE ARE SAYING ABOUT

SPIRITED NATURE

Simon's beautifully written tale is breathtakingly evocative of rural Irish life – the sounds, smells, colours, pace, and bucolic atmosphere are lovingly summoned to vibrant life on the page.

Yet this is no ordinary tale of pastoral living. It is Simon's shamanic encounters with Herne and other denizens of liminal realms and the deceptive ease with which he walks between the worlds that make this a remarkable account of a life-changing experience, one that forces us to question our own relationships with other beings and the very nature of reality.

Grahame Gardner, President of the British Society of Dowsers

Spirited Nature

Healing adventures in rural Ireland

Spirited Nature

Healing adventures in
rural Ireland

Simon Gordon Wheeler

BOOKS

Winchester, UK
Washington, USA

First published by O-Books, 2014
O-Books is an imprint of John Hunt Publishing Ltd., Laurel House, Station Approach,
Alresford, Hants, SO24 9JH, UK
office1@jhpbooks.net
www.johnhuntpublishing.com

For distributor details and how to order please visit the 'Ordering' section on our website.

Text copyright: Simon Gordon Wheeler 2013

ISBN: 978 1 78279 319 9

A CIP catalogue record for this book is available from the British Library.

Design: Stuart Davies

Printed in the USA by Edwards Brothers Malloy

We operate a distinctive and ethical publishing philosophy in all areas of our business, from our global network of authors to production and worldwide distribution.

CONTENTS

Preface

Thank you for choosing this book.

I did not write this as a 'self-help' book. Of course, you may find, when you have finished it, that it does help you in some way.

It is not an autobiography. The stories may be in part about me and some of my experiences, but only as a brief snapshot of a few years in my more than 60 of life.

It is not fiction. These things did happen. It would be fair to say that this is not a verbatim record: I rely on my memory. It's as accurate as I can get, although I have changed names of places and people.

So, if those are what it's not, what is it then?

It just *is*.

My little inner voice nagged me for years: should I be a psychic medium? Or a healer? In which case, animals or people? Or both? Or should I be a shaman? Or a clairvoyant? Or a professional dowser? Or work as a remote viewer? Or…? Or any other 'label'. The answer is: yes and no. Be all of these things. And more. But above all, *just be*.

So, now I try to just be. And this book just is.

I hope you enjoy it.

There are relevant photographs, information and some pages of resources on my website.

www.simongordonwheeler.co.uk

Introduction

These tales are set in the Wicklow Mountains. It doesn't matter exactly where. But what does matter is to have some sort of understanding of what the environment is like, especially if, like me, you are a townie from England; or a "blow-in" as outsiders are called around here.

Towns and cities are man-made. The mountains are Nature-made, and are aeons older than any of us. They have a power and a presence all of their own. They remind us of our insignificance: of our temporary and transitory existence. Whilst some of the local farmers may try to claim back the bracken-covered hillsides, and squabble over grazing rights, the bottom line is that within each hilltop, within each mountain, there is a unique voice: a voice so deep it is beyond the hearing of human beings. And on the surface the faces of these mountains are always changing: working with, and in response to, the weather, the seasons, the time of day and the phases of the moon.

When the moon is new and the clouds cover the stars in the winter nights, the blackness is immense. There are no shadows, no silhouettes, no forms to be discerned looming out of the darkness. When the moon is full and the clouds are chasing the sky in another part of the world, it is light enough to read a book at midnight. And when there is the intermediate stage: some moon, a few clouds and starlight, the world takes on an eerie form. It becomes grey and misty, formless, smoothed and unsubstantiated, yet still alive with the watcher's perceptions of what is known to be there in daylight: the trees, the streams, the fields, the lanes, hedges and stone walls.

In daytime the shapes shift and the colours move in response to the light. The sunrise reds and russet browns on the hills on the horizon will meld into greens and dark browns, as the day grows older and longer. The shadows will emphasise the distant trees and the dots that are sheep and cattle a half a mile or so across the valley. The wind will find little resistance in the branches of the ash and the oak; the conifers in plantations will stand guard over the hillside, until the loggers come with their enormous noisy machines and reduce them to poles and timber lengths; and then their offspring will be planted and the cycle begins again.

The sound of rooks and sheep and cattle dominate. Sometimes you might hear the trickle of the stream in the garden, or an occasional car driving along the lane. The tractors' engines move in and out of your consciousness. At night there is silence. Real silence. Silence that reminds you that the nearest human neighbours are out of sight and out of earshot; that reminds you that you are a being living in the midst of the vastness of Nature. That you are small and, as the Bible says, a speck of dust.

It seems that within the mountains there are several microclimates. It is possible to leave home, home being a cottage with half an acre of land, goats, chickens, guinea fowl and ducks, and two cats, and be in the midst of lashing rain and gale-force winds. Behind us is the Big Meadow: a large field that slopes down to our boundary fencing; where Padraig, our immediate neighbour and farmer, keeps either cattle or sheep, depending upon the time of year and state of the weather. Padraig's land surrounds us. One of his sons, Jimmy, lives a few hundred yards away from us; his garden, which is a field really, is adjacent to our boundary wall. We can see beyond Padraig's land to the pointy mountain, in the shelter of which, across the valley, live our friends Don and Jane Crowne. A few miles down the road, in the village, it is sunny and still. Driving the twelve miles to the nearest town you can pass through rain, sun, rain again; roads suddenly edging from wet to dry and back to wet.

There is no mains water or gas to the cottage. We drink water that is piped from a stream up the mountainside via a deep well. The well serves four houses and sometimes can run low; but the water is soft and pure. Heating is from a solid fuel stove. We do not have a collection service for the trash; we burn what will burn and bundle the rest into old fertiliser bags and take it to the council tip once every few months.

Driving along the potholed lanes at night you may see a fox or the lights from the reflected eyes of a deer; there are hares, hordes of rabbits and pheasant, grouse and partridge. In the autumn and winter the Dublin men are out lamping on quad bikes or in 4 X 4 vehicles, guns at the ready. The rutting stags bellow at night from the boggy woods in the dip at the bottom of the field over the road. The bats flit through the air.

Time is different here. It has another way of floating in the background of our lives. It is not tight and linear, but loose and flexible. The days are the length that they are, as are the nights. The dawn breaks when it will and dusk advances to its own, ever-changing, rules. For there are no rules here. Perhaps this is why the people are so laid back. Artificial structures are irrelevant. Life is as it is: things happen in the way that they do. Priorities, if they exist at all, are not the priorities of the British rat race. Gossip is a major currency here. But then so are humour, mutual support and friendship – once you are known and some trust develops. There is a paradox: the social world here is parochial and insular at times, yet the physical world seems boundless. There can be smallness within the hugeness.

First time visitors remark upon the emptiness. And the varying hues of green. Green is everywhere. No wonder this is the Emerald Isle. For not only is it green, it is a jewel. A precious stone set in God's sea. Of course, this is, prosaically, mostly due to the rain. But even on the greyest and most brutal of days, the land sparkles its greenery, the shades deepening in the brief intervals of dryness.

Winters are grim. And long. Sometimes the snow diverts attention, but mostly it is the rain, and the wind, that dominate. Roads are potholed and gritty with detritus washed from the farmland. The livestock huddles under trees or in the shelter of boundaries, waiting for respite from the chill and the wet. The grass becomes mud. Rivers and streams suddenly become empowered, swirling and racing down mountainsides. Waterfalls spume and roar from the craggy peaks that overlook glaciated valleys. Life is harsh and slow and feels as if it is to be endured rather than to be appreciated as a joy.

But when the birds start to build nests; when the hens and ducks begin their season of egg laying; when the lambs start to appear in the fields and the plants and trees awaken again, as they invariably do – then we know that Nature's cycle is ceaseless, however dulled our spirits may have become.

And this is what this story is about: spirit. A much misused and misunderstood word. And concept.

While, at times, living here can seem to sap our spirits, sometimes the energies seem stagnant: digging below the surface reveals a spirituality of the earth. Man is a physical being. We are here to live our lives. And in these parts, living life is a true balancing act. Nature is manipulated through our use of the land. Yet the land will always be in control. It is part of Nature, literally and metaphorically, its bedrock. Of course, we like to believe we can use, though some would say abuse, the land for our own benefit. To an extent we can. Just as when our hen or duck eggs hatch and there are too many males, a cull is necessary. To leave an excess of cockerels or drakes is cruel: the lives of the female of the species are made terrible. But that's the way we manage domesticated life. Wildlife evens *itself* out. The Seamus Heaney poem comes to mind: "The Early Purges" – the one about rural life, where he writes that there is no room for sentiment in the countryside.

Our cats will bring home their prey: usually baby rabbits. The cats are so proud. If the rabbit is still alive its squeaking is like nails scratching on a blackboard. But to 'rescue' the rabbit is to doom it to a life of pain and starvation; for as soon as the cat has caught it and brought it home there is no hope. All we can do is wait. And clean up the uneaten parts. But even these can be hurled over the hedge where they will be fodder for some other creatures. The same is true for when we see a duck waddle past with a squirming frog protruding from its mouth. Nothing is wasted.

For someone unaccustomed to such apparent barbarity: Nature in the raw, tooth and claw, it is not always easy to adjust. But adjustment is necessary. We learn to respect the ways of the earth. When a ewe is lambing the chances are she will manage to give birth on her own. But, sometimes, a little help is required. And livestock is no respecter of fencing and artificial boundaries. Our poultry wanders into a neighbour's meadow; his sheep, and sometimes cattle, wander across our lawn. When we grow crops we ensure the soil is in good order. Crops are rotated to maintain nutrients; and when nutrients are depleted we artificially restore them by adding whatever we believe is necessary. So, Man and Nature sometimes work hand-in-hand, sometimes in conflict. Any farmer will know that if in conflict it is Nature that, ultimately, will win. *Our* time on this earth is short; Nature endures.

It is, then, within this context that my story is set. A context of the natural world that we cannot always explain and certainly do not completely understand; but a world in which we strive to live harmoniously; in which growth, death and birth, and mystery, are all a vital part of our experience.

Chapter One

Circe is a black and white British Alpine goat. She and her mother, Sweetie, are residents in our paddock. They have a wooden shed for shelter, plenty of grass upon which to graze, and are like pets. Circe was born here about 12 years ago. She loves being brushed and the top of her head scratched. When the weather is fine we take her and tether her on a long rope at the side of one of the lanes. Then she can browse: eating ferns, brambles, blackthorn, ash tree leaves – whatever she can reach. Sweetie will eat thistles too, but as she is in her mid-twenties she is a dowager goat. She knows her own mind and can, literally, dig in her heels if she does not want to do anything.

We take Circe for walks, as if she were a dog. On a long leash we trek the lanes, pausing at the verge (the "long mile" they call that here) to snack. When we crest the brow of the hill and the cottage is in sight on the way back, Circe will trot. Then gallop. It keeps us fit.

She also likes to play. Chasing her around the paddock, she will leap the stream and tear into the lambing pen, glancing behind to make sure she is being followed. Once in the pen she will pretend to be cornered and then race out the gate. It can be exhausting. Her favourite is to be pushed. If you press hard with the palm of your hand on to the top of her head, emulating a goat butt, she will rise on to her back legs and pretend to threaten. Her front legs will be curled back, then wave at you; her ears will be high and held back and the hair on her spine stands on end. I have watched her do this to intruding dogs. The goat wins.

Usually dogs are not a problem, but sometimes a walker passes by and their dog sees and hears the hens and ducks and seems to think of them as either playmates or easy game. Sometimes the poultry stands transfixed, sometimes they run. Circe will always bleat loudly. When the goat bleats and hens and ducks kick up a fuss, it is wise to investigate. The best warning comes from the guinea fowl. Unfortunately they can give alarm calls for something they see a long way off: any unusual shape, noise or unknown person can give rise to terrible shrieking.

I described Circe as more like a pet. Not quite the same can be said for the birds, but there are always some which seem to be more interesting, attractive or full of character than others. For example, at the moment (for birds have a relatively short life), there is Spangles. She is a real 'tea cosy' hen and was hatched here. She always was her own hen, preferring to keep her own company, rather than run with her hatch mates. What has made her a little special is her propensity not to go into the shed at night unless she is picked up and placed inside the henhouse door. She waits for all the others to go in, watches you arrive in the paddock to close the henhouse and then sort of settles on her haunches. She chirrups as she is picked up.

Then there is one of the guinea fowl. He has been here for several years but when we bought in some new hens from a breeder near Dublin he took to one of these hens. Now the two of them spend all day going everywhere together. The guinea spends nights roosting in a tree, but just before it is time to let out the hens in the morning he will fly down and sit outside the henhouse door. It's rather like a child calling on a friend to come out to play.

We hatched a bantam recently. We call her "Tweetie Pie" after the cartoon bird. She runs like a velociraptor and behaves like an objectionable adolescent... hassling all the other birds at feeding time but running back to 'Mum' when she gets stamped on by a resident duck that will not tolerate such presumptuous behaviour.

At feeding time the phrase 'pecking order' is made explicit. However, we do get wild birds coming to the troughs. Rooks abound nearby and often have to be hissed away when the poultry have finished. Sometimes a wild pheasant will come trundling down the hillside and tentatively feed.

When you keep poultry you are a target for foxes. And there are many of them around here. It is quite common to see cubs, or even full-grown foxes, splatted on one of the nearby roads or lanes. Just above the cottage seems to be a fox run: where they descend from the mountainside, cross the road and head towards a wooded bog. If they mistime their crossing of the road, and cars can come around the corner pretty quickly, then they are killed. This can also happen to our birds.

We have dozens of ducks and hens; we sell their eggs. We have several hatches of eggs a year: provided there is a broody bird to sit on a clutch. Neighbours share broody birds. We borrow a hen from someone, eggs hatch: and a hen will hatch any hen's, or duck's, eggs; and the hen is returned with some of the progeny. It works well. However, there does come a time when inbreeding can be an issue. Hence a widespread network of poultry keepers develops.

Breeding your own birds is fine, provided you don't mind mongrel offspring, but buying them in keeps the gene pool fresh. However, it can be expensive. It is debatable which is worse: having spent money on buying birds and seeing them taken by the fox, or the fox taking birds bred at home. It is almost impossible to provide fox-proof fencing, especially if the birds are free range. Again, it is all part of the natural world. Nevertheless, you resent providing easy food for the local fox population.

So, what can be done?

Shooting is a possibility. But foxes are not easy to shoot with a shotgun, which is what is locked away in the gun cabinet in the cottage. You have to get really close. We don't have a rifle. Of course, shooting can result in a wounded animal and that is cruel, as trapping can be, even if the fox had decimated our flocks. I did once track down a fox lair on the hillside behind the cottage. I had permission from our neighbour, a farmer who owns the land, to shoot the fox. Foxes, and mink, can take lambs. But when I went up the mountain and saw the dog fox sitting at the edge of the field I could not bring myself to even raise the gun. It was a fabulous animal. It didn't help that he just sat there and eyeballed me. Perhaps he knew. After a few minutes he just slouched off into the bushes and I came home. It made me think.

I took the gun, locked it back in the cabinet, and sat on the bench outside the cottage watching the birds in and around the paddock. There had to be another way. I found I was daydreaming, sitting there in the early spring sunshine. I could hear the stream gently trickling and the rooks in the trees. The hens and ducks were mostly just enjoying the sun – some dust-bathing in bits of dirt. I closed my eyes and let myself drift, the bright light almost penetrating my eyelids. I had recently become more effective at meditation; this was a quiet place in which to learn; in which to *"switch off your mind, relax and float downstream"*: as the Beatles had sung decades ago.

With my eyes gently closed I started to see a figure on horseback. He appeared as if out of a mist, riding towards me. On his head was an imposing and impressive set of antlers; his face was masked. The mist turned red and orange, as he seemed to burst out of a huge set of flames and rode up to face me. He stopped right in front of where I sat. He laughed. Still I kept my eyes closed. And still he, and the horse, were there. He rode around the cottage and our land and disappeared. As he rode back into the flames he waved his right arm in a friendly gesture of farewell.

In some ways it seemed very real; but I couldn't help wonder if the flames were a result of my closed eyes in the sunlight, a physical effect. He had seemed familiar: some sort of mythical or legendary figure; but who he was I couldn't recall and what he wanted I had no idea. In some ways it was an extraordinary experience; yet it felt quite normal.

I opened my eyes and was almost surprised that everything was as it had been before I had sat down. But, sure enough, the poultry were still scratching and dust-bathing and the goats still grazing in the paddock. The stream still trickled and the lambs still played racing games in the field behind us. I stood up and stretched. Feeling somewhat foolish I looked around for telltale signs of my visitor. I don't know what I was looking for, what I expected to see, but I looked anyway. I leaned on the paddock gate and watched the hens and ducks. I jumped over the stream to gaze at the lambs. I ambled around the place, picking up twigs from under the ash trees and kicking clumps of grass. I could not get the picture out of my mind.

I crossed the road opposite our front lawn and climbed Padraig's sheep fence into his field opposite. About a hundred yards in front of me now, at the bottom of the sloping field, was the "bog". This was an area of shrub, scrub, trees and very heavy mossy ground shielding a small river: home to various wildlife and a place of almost complete serenity. The river ran parallel to the road for a couple of miles and the bogland extended for anywhere between fifty and two hundred yards either side of the water. In the winter your wellies would get sucked knee-deep into the ground if you dared venture too close to the river at certain points; in the summer it was just a case of ducking and weaving through brambles, fallen trees, woodland and scrub.

The field was empty of livestock so I was completely alone. In fact, now I think of it, there was no sound either – no rooks, no tractors, no cars. I was in my own little bubble.

I walked on down to the treeline. Everywhere was quite still. No breeze lifted the leaves or disturbed the grass. No bird wings sucked and blew the air in the sky. I had to stop. I had to stand immobile. I don't know why, but I did.

And so I stood there. Alone. Fixed to the ground. Silent. Lost in time. Breathing ever so gently so as not to burst my bubble. There but not there. Me but not me. Looking at nothing really. My eyes saw the hills, saw the sky, saw the trees where the hill and sky overlapped; saw the trees where the grass formed the base of the landscape. But I was doing more than seeing: I was belonging. Maybe I should be self-conscious, pretentious even, with my use of words here. Because it was not just belonging. It was being and longing.

It must have been my transition back to self-consciousness, my realisation that I was, in some way, daydreaming, that made me slowly turn. I looked up towards the road, towards where I had come from, the top of the field. Sprinting right at me was a hare. He bounded over the ruts, leapt over the knolls and headed straight at me. I had no idea what to do; though why I thought I needed to do anything I can't imagine. He really didn't seem to know I was there. Then, about six feet away from me, he stopped. He paused. He leaned back on his haunches. I could make out every detail of his body, the markings on his fur. He looked straight at me. I was reminded of my encounter with the dog fox: eyeball to eyeball. And then he took off again. Bounding into the woodland now behind me, he was gone. The whole thing was over in a few seconds; yet the incident seemed, like the previous half-hour or so, strangely profound.

I followed in his tracks and headed down to the river. The briars and bracken were not yet a barrier, so it was quite easy to pick up the sheep and deer paths that led to the water.

The river is only about five yards wide as it tumbles over the rocks and flows across pools that are millennia old yet ever-changing. The water is clean and the depth not great, so that stones and pebbles on its bed can be discerned beneath the bubbling and rolling ripples. As the sun shines through the guardian trees, the tint of the water takes on russets and gentle rusty browns, as well as reflecting the many hues of green it collects from leaves and grass and moss and plants.

And now I sit on the edge of the water, staring into its hypnotic wakes. The images, both real and imagined, of the last hour or so keep resurfacing, like the tumbling twigs that I can see the river carry from bend to bend, pool to pool. Again I am aware of my own bubble – separate from Time and a pinprick in Space. I don't know how long I sat. It could have been a few seconds, it could have been many minutes. But eventually I stood up and headed back to the cottage.

I felt at peace as I tramped up the slope towards the field. I got to the edge of the trees and went through a different gap to head home. I could hear our cockerels crowing; first the hens and then the higher pitch of the bantams. I also heard movement much closer – in the trees to my left and slightly behind me. I stopped and turned. There stood a deer. She was about twenty feet from me. This was proving to be one amazing day! However, unlike the hare, she did not hang about. A quick twitch of the head and she rushed into the shelter and safety of the woods.

Back at the cottage I put the kettle on. It seemed a sort of normal thing to do.

As I stood in the kitchen waiting for the water to boil, the phone rang. It was Jane Crowne. She and Don have a small farm across the valley from us. They're about 10 minutes' drive away; much of that time being spent very carefully negotiating the potholes on their half-mile long drive. Jane is English but Don is a 'West Brit': Irish by birth but generations back an English 'gentleman' and landowner who encouraged the feudal system in Ireland and kept the natives gainfully employed while enjoying a rather more comfortable lifestyle. Or at least that's how some would see it. 'West Brit' is a rather derogatory term for anyone of Anglo-Irish descent; possibly referring to those who once saw Ireland as a sort of Western Britain. Anyway, more of Jane and Don later.

Jane also keeps hens and ducks and we sell her eggs for her. When she can find them. Her poultry lays anywhere on the farm, so unless somebody scales the hay and straw bales of both barns and scours the stables, let alone treks the fields near to the house or rummages in the garden, it is a matter of luck whether or not eggs are uncovered.

She phones us once or twice a week. And we do the same for them. It's just a way of keeping in touch. It could be a lonely and isolated life in this part of the world. Though she can be wearing; even her phone chats are somewhat frenetic and all over the place. It's like she saves up all her thoughts and energies and then spews them out in as short a time as possible. She also calls in sometimes when passing the cottage, which she does to get to the village. And the fact that we share English ancestry, and common acquaintances back in the UK, accelerated the forming of bonds between us all.

As we were chatting, and I was making my tea while the phone was precariously perched between cheek and shoulder, I was wondering whether or not to either tell her about my afternoon, or at least ask her about the figure on horseback. Jane is quite comfortable with most things. I suppose as a farmer's wife (though she's much more than that) you have to be, but she also has strong opinions and can be very single-minded. She is well-educated and well read, although she did talk too much for my liking about Rudolf Steiner. So I asked her, making out that I'd had a dream. Which it had seemed like, so that wasn't too difficult to do.

"Oh yes," she said. "That sounds like Herne the Hunter. The Irish call him Cernunnos, but I think you'll find it's the same thing. I wonder why you dreamed about him."

I had a choice to make. So I told her: it's no good having friends if you can't trust them. I told her the truth about the afternoon's events.

"Oh you are lucky," was her response. "Gosh. I wish something like that would happen to me. We've always had problems with foxes here, as you know. In fact I think I lost two hens last night. Brendan promised to set traps on the mountain and to ask Michael to bring his rifle across."

Which got me thinking. Why did it all happen to *me*? When Jane had finished, and I felt a little bit calmer, I sat in the Family

Room with the patio doors open and sipped my tea. I could see the hens squabbling and the ducks marching in single file up the Big Meadow; I considered the afternoon's events.

It had really all started when I stomped up the hill behind us with the shotgun to take out the local fox. And, if you'll excuse the pun, I 'chickened out'. Perhaps that was it. My encounters with the hare and deer were reminders of the… well, I don't know what. The magic of Nature perhaps? The right that animals have to live their own lives? OK. They live their own lives but what about when their lives encroach on ours? Why are we always so quick to solve the problem with a drastic solution, the ultimate answer: to kill? Maybe Herne/Cernunnos was showing me that there's another way. I knew we couldn't fox-proof the paddock. I wasn't going to kill the foxes. What else was there? He seemed friendly and cheery enough. Perhaps his wave goodbye wasn't that at all. I felt shivers and goose bumps as the next thought overtook me: perhaps he was inviting me to follow him. Or to ask him for help. Help that he would be happy to give.

That was it. Somehow I actually knew that was it. He was there to help. All I had to do was ask.

OK. So exactly how do you ask a mythical figure to help? And if you don't know how to ask, who can you ask to help you ask? This was tricky. And distinctly weird.

I went outside again and sat on my bench overlooking the paddock. I took a deep breath and closed my eyes. Nothing. Nobody. No horse, no mist, no fire. No Cernunnos. I opened my eyes. And closed them once more. This time I concentrated and tried hard to draw back to me the image of a few hours previous. I lifted my head up so that my eyelids could feel the warmth of the sun and detect the rose-pink hues. Rather than looking at the back of my eyelids I looked through and beyond. And I silently asked for help, for guidance, for assurance. I focussed my attention some distance away from me, but still with my eyes gently closed. And I heard the sound of hooves. Startled now, I opened my eyes and looked around. This was new. But nothing was there. Eyes shut. Back to my focussing again, and almost immediately he was back. The horse reared in front of me: black and shiny, glossy and magnificent. With Cernunnos leaning back, reins in his left hand, a fist raised with his right. This time, though, there was a pack of hounds following behind. Their mouths were open as if barking, but I could hear no sounds. And suddenly they were gone. All of them. Vanished.

I suppose if I were a child I would see this as some sort of magical game. *"Close your eyes and meet the Hunter."* But this was real. Well... perhaps. Define 'real'! Anyway, I suppose I could sit and see what happened over the next few minutes if I kept concentrating and opening and closing my eyes. But now I had an indication; now I had more information. Now I could see what it was I had to do. In some way I felt quite elated. This was good. This was fun. Working with/playing with, figures from... well... from a mystical realm I suppose. And I didn't feel in the least bit that I was going mad or that this was silly. It all seemed very natural. Because that's what it was. A natural way to deal with the fox problem. But for now it would have to wait until dusk.

Perhaps at this point it would be sensible to fill in a bit more background. After all, I have been writing "our" and "we" and not explained who else may be involved here. Her name is Sally. It is her cottage; her poultry; her goats. She and I have known one another for about 35 years. It is only recently that we have lived together: we both had divorces a good many years back; both had other long-term relationships. She moved here 15 years ago. Why I moved here a few months ago to be with her is in a later chapter.

Sally now works in a factory that makes breast implants. She works in quality control. Perhaps I could make facetious or risqué comments about this; but of course I won't. She works a day shift one week, followed by evenings the next week, followed by a night shift in week three. She's only been doing this a short while and so we are both getting used to it. When I first arrived she was not working, so I was able to pick up the routine and procedures for looking after all the creatures while she was around. I had had no experience of smallholding work. I'd once owned a cat. Oh, and a hamster when I was about ten. But two goats, two cats, two guinea fowl, twenty ducks and twenty hens: this was something else. And I loved it. It was certainly different from my day job as a teacher/counsellor.

There was always something that needed doing: cleaning out sheds, or mending them; buying feed from the local Co-operative store; visiting a local farm to negotiate a price for straw or hay bales; and then putting them in the trailer and driving back home; splitting logs for the stove; in the summer cutting grass and in the winter sorting out drainage problems; mending fences; grooming the goats or taking them for a walk. And these were the routine tasks; you never knew when something unexpected would require time, money and energy.

Sally was due home soon. I would talk with her about what happened and the next possible step. But now it was getting distinctly cold outside. I went back into the cottage through the patio doors, shutting them behind me. I put the kettle on so that when Sally got back she'd not have to wait long for a drink. At the same time, I collected a bowl from the kitchen and went back outside.

As I opened the paddock gate all the birds came scurrying around my feet as usual. They knew it was feeding time. But they should also have known that the feed went in their troughs, and there was no point in running to me. In some ways hens and ducks appear quite intelligent; in other ways, not at all. When it comes to food: it's the "not at all".

I put the empty bowl on the grass. The hens tried pecking it. Opening the door to the feed shed, I had to shoo away a few of the cheekier birds before shutting the bottom half of the door; it's a stable door arrangement. I scooped the layers' pellets and crushed wheat from the plastic dustbins into the feed pans. By now the noise outside the shed resembled an avian equivalent of a children's party where 4 year olds squabbled over pass-the-parcel or musical chairs.

As I walked up the paddock to the troughs I must have looked like the Pied Piper. I emptied the feed along all four troughs and made my escape. The birds pushed, pecked, squawked and dashed around – as always.

I replaced the feed pans in the shed, shut the door and picked up the bowl from the grass, and went to check the nesting boxes for any more eggs. I'd already collected a dozen first thing this morning, but often there's a few more during the day. The ducks, though, tended only to lay just before they are let out first thing in the morning. The ducks lay their eggs on the straw in their house; so when the door is opened in the morning and they storm out of their shed, any eggs laid loose near the door can be trampled on. Though most of the time they make nests near the side or back of the shed.

I collected two hen eggs and was heading back to the cottage when I heard Sally's car come down the hill and into the driveway by the back door. I crossed the front lawn but had to stop. The sun was setting behind the pointy mountain. I stood and watched as the sky in front of me displayed a palette of reds and browns and pinks and yellows and purples and oranges: all shifting and melding, merging and melting – tingeing the grass, trees and bracken with the most extraordinary light. Light which you could almost reach out and touch: but touching wouldn't be enough. Light which you could hold in your hands, which you could drink, which was hypnotic, which was fragrant.

It probably only lasted a minute or two. I have no idea. But when I emerged from my little dream I noticed that now the clouds were looking ominous and yellow. I took my bowl and went in to see Sally.

It was a relief to leave the cold air behind as I went into the kitchen. Sally was nowhere to be seen, but the kettle was boiling again. I guessed she would be in the bedroom at the back of the cottage, changing from her work clothes. So I made two mugs of tea and took them into the lounge.

"Hi," I heard the call from our bedroom.

"Hi. How was work?"

"Much as usual." The footsteps along the wooden floor of the corridor between lounge and bedroom got louder. I stood up and kissed her as she arrived, tucking a shirt into her jeans under the fleece. "Knackered as ever. Thanks for the cuppa... that's great."

"OK."

We sat in silence for a while, sipping at tea, each lost in our own thoughts; but comfortable with that.

The catflap banged open and shut: Dizzy had heard the car and arrived home to say hello and check his food bowl. Which he did. Of course, all this time Winston, our other cat, was asleep on one of the armchairs.

"Shall I light the fire?"

"That'd be good. On the way home they said on the radio it might snow tonight."

"Ah." Now that would be interesting. I'd have to think about that. Anyway, for now I needed to collect the twigs from the box in the back porch and set the fire.

After a few minutes the window of the stove showed a healthy flickering red glow. You always knew when the fire had caught properly because the cats would start to edge closer. If it was likely to go out, or need replenishing with coal or logs too quickly, Dizzy and Winston would be reluctant to give up their sleeping spot in case a human sat there.

I wondered what to do about Cernunnos if snow was due. I wanted to have it clear in my mind before I told Sally what had occurred during the afternoon.

"My turn to put the birds to bed?" she asked, putting down

her now empty mug.

"I don't mind doing it."

"Neither do I. Anyway, I want to check the shed doors; one seems knackered and might need mending. You know I like pottering when I get back."

"Yeah, I know. But it's getting a bit bloody cold for pottering."

"That's what jackets are for."

So, Sally donned one of her padded zip-ups, a woolly hat, welly boots and ventured out to the paddock. It gave me time to wash the mugs and to think.

I went back into the lounge and turned on the TV. We had to have satellite television because there was no other way of getting reception; the hills and mountains blocked the signal. I had thought about putting an aerial way up in the top of one of the trees in the Big Meadow, but my wish to prevent Mr Murdoch getting more of my money than necessary was super-seded by a pragmatic attitude. So now I zapped through the channels to check out the weather forecast. Sure enough, snow was due. But that wasn't surprising, considering the colour of the sky and clouds at sunset.

I checked the stove would last a while... upsetting the cats when I opened the door as they were lying on the hearthrug in luxurious contemplation. I, too, then dressed for the weather and ventured outside. I knew Sally treasured her time pottering and enjoyed doing it alone; but this time I had to explain before embarking on my experiment. She knew I meditated and she was tolerant and understanding of my occasionally fey behaviour. But we had only briefly discussed what these days some would call "New Age stuff": largely because it was new to me, seemed quite natural and normal and was part of daily life. It was in part what had brought me here. Anyway, I found "New Age" to be a rather insulting epithet for something that probably stretched back further than we knew and the phrase was associated with things that did not necessarily have the integrity to which I aspired. I mustn't rant; and more will become clear as these stories unfold.

Dusk was starting to cover our little world. I could hear the poultry flapping and complaining as Sally moved them into their sheds. The hens would squabble about who perched where and when. If they felt hard done by, or found they were not going to bed in what they perceived as the right order, they would go into the shed, turn around and come straight back out again. Then others would follow; so just as you thought they were all safely in, they'd start 'leaking' out. The problem was that if they were left to their own devices, some would elect not to go into the shed for the night and try sleeping in the goat shed. Which made them vulnerable to foxes. It was often easier to have two people herding the hens, although sometimes this would confuse the birds even more. Hens can move pretty quickly. One way of discouraging them, and using their limited intellect to your advantage, is to make yourself appear larger. So it is not unusual to see either Sally or myself shouting (or more likely swearing) at hens, with our arms outstretched doing aeroplane impressions. Failing that, grabbing a long stick in each hand, thus extending our own 'wings', and bearing down upon the unfortunate bird, or birds, usually worked. But what passers-by thought I have no idea. It was perhaps fortunate that there were so few. Or perhaps those that knew us just chose to see it as another example of "*the mad British*" in action.

The ducks were a little better to deal with. They wouldn't even consider going to bed unless they were already lined up in the correct order a few yards from their shed. And had circled it several times, just to make sure it actually was their shed. The problem with the ducks was getting them anywhere near their shed when they'd rather be in the Big Meadow dabbling for worms and insects. Sometimes calling "duckduckduck- duckduck" at the right pitch and volume would encourage them to look up, shake themselves and fall into rank before wobbling into the paddock and across the stream. When calling them worked, it was most impressive. It seemed to me just like having a trained sheepdog. Though I now suspect that they were humouring me, rather than being acquiescent.

So, by now Sally was closing the doors on the ducks, the hens having already been persuaded in. The goats had paid no attention whatsoever. Occasionally one, or both, would stop whatever was receiving their attention at the time and enjoy the performance. Indeed, it was not unknown for them to contribute to the 'fun'. Especially Circe. When the time came for the birds to be put away Circe might be found standing right in front of the hen sheds. This meant that the birds would have to run under her body and between her legs. Fine for them, and for her. But not for us. It just contributed to the chaos. I would get most of the birds in and then grab Circe by the collar (she always wore a collar so that we could attach a tether to her) to lead her off. She'd dig her heels in, just for the hell of it, and then move off into the middle of the paddock. By then the birds which had been in had come out, and those that were thinking of going in had run off to hide: under the straw bale, behind the shed, in the hedge – wherever. So start again. Strangely, though, Circe seemed to know when this game of hers was not going to be tolerated: for example, when we wanted to go out for the evening and didn't want to be late. Then she would stand a little further away from the shed. She would wait until most birds were on their perches and when she felt the time was right she'd begin to casually walk after those that were left outside near the door. As I aeroplaned towards the shed the birds that appeared ready to give themselves up as fox meat, Circe would walk the closer ones to their door. And then she'd step aside until all were safely gathered in. This behaviour of hers always resulted in an extra ration of nuts for her; but even though she may have seen this as a reward, if she ever didn't want to cooperate she obviously was happy to forego her reward, apparently getting more satisfaction out of being stroppy. But that's goats for you.

As Sally slid the catch on the last door a snowflake passed in front of me. Then another, then another. They were the big, soft, floaty flakes rather than the scratchy, pellety impoverished flakes that you sometimes get in winter. I had to tell Sally what I was doing, and tell her quickly: neither of us would want to stay outside too long in this weather, especially as the fire was lit.

"I'm staying out for a few more minutes," I told her. "I have some work to do."

"OK. What is it?"

"Fox protection."

"We'll see if they're around in the morning, if this keeps up. The tracks will be clear as anything."

"I know. That's why I want to do it now."

"Do what? Exactly?"

"Can I tell you when I'm done? It's a long story."

"OK then. That's grand. I'm going in. It's getting heavier. And darker."

As Sally huddled off into the growing darkness and into the cottage, I decided that I'd start at the road. I went through the paddock gate, following Sally, but then went across the lawn and on to the road. I was at one corner of our land.

I heard Sally open the back door, saw the light briefly and then heard the door close, leaving me in darkness again. I stood in the road and concentrated. I tried to stay relaxed but also fix my mind on Cernunnos. It was not easy maintaining a picture of him, his horse and the hounds when snow kept brushing my face. After a few seconds I felt his presence, his form was taking shape. Then, with a whooosh, he was here. Stunning antlers on his head, his horse shining and proud. And the dogs. The all-important dogs.

I thanked him for being with me. Aloud I asked him to walk with me. I set off down the road, my mystical and invisible entourage beside me. The hounds seemed impatient, the horse restless. I felt I should be running so that they would be happier with the pace. But I walked. I walked to the next corner of our land. And there I stood, asking for protection from Herne the Hunter and his hounds: protection for all living creatures within the boundaries we were marking.

By now I was feeling a bit calmer. I realised that the first couple of times I'd seen Herne/Cernunnos I was intimidated by the thought and feeling of his power. As I stood at the second 'Marker' I felt this less so. He was no more, or less, powerful than I was. We were working together in partnership. Equally respectful of each other. But how it had come to this, and why, I had no idea.

I climbed from the road, up the bank and hopped over our fence. I had to decide where to walk now. Should I take us all into the Big Meadow, or keep the boundary of protection inside our own fencing? I decided upon the latter. It would be easier to 'top up', whatever that meant. I was now knowing things but not knowing how I knew. It was as if I was communicating not only with Herne/Cernunnos but also others, and doing so telepathically. Communicating was, perhaps, not the right concept. Because I was not really aware that I was giving or receiving information and ideas – they were just 'there'. Wherever 'there' was.

So now I asked again for his protection. I specified the poultry and the goats, as well as for all living creatures. I did wonder if that would be taken literally: what about all the insects, for example? The worms? The frogs in the stream? But I felt that what I wanted was known, that I had to conduct this ritual to make concrete the abstraction of my intentions. And that I had to believe that what was right would be so.

We all stopped at the third point of the journey around the land. I knew that the ducks went into the Meadow. I knew they would now be safe there and that I would have to have faith. I could not ask for protection for the whole of the Big Meadow.

That would be asking too much of Herne and too much of the foxes. For somehow Herne was not the Hunter but the intermediary. He was the persuader, not the killer. He would not be killing the foxes for me. Killing was not right. That is why he is here. We share the same goal: live and let live. Foxes have to eat. But my intentions, my values, my wish to find another way, were being attended to. There was plenty of food out on the mountainside; the foxes would just have to work a little harder. Otherwise they'd have the hounds after them. If the foxes crossed the boundaries of protection, they would be chased away.

It was then that I noticed that I hadn't noticed the birds. Normally, when walking past or even close to the poultry sheds at night, there'd be noise. It might be warning noises, a cockerel crowing or it might be light chirruping. The ducks would seem to shift position and scuffle, with an occasional quack of complaint. But even though I'd walked right next to them, they had all been silent.

Now I was at the final corner, where the stream tumbled down the mountain, through the fence and on to our land. I could see Sally in the kitchen, from where the light spilled on to the grassy bank by the steps that lead up to the washing line. I stood again for a few seconds, giving my thanks and asking for protection. I walked down the slope, past the back door and paused at exactly the same point from where I had begun. I asked that the protection be given within the boundaries we had marked and promised that I would walk them again every week. That was my commitment.

Cernunnos raised a gloved hand – I hadn't seen the glove previously – and beckoned the hounds. They raced in front of him as he dug his heels into his horse's flank and they all set off towards the pointy mountain. I waved as they left. Although it was dark they still seemed to leave a silhouette as they got further away. I sent them my thanks. And I stood there while the snow gathered on the grass.

I became conscious that I was very cold. So I turned back to the cottage and retreated inside to the warmth of the fire and the sound of repeats of *The Bill* on TV.

"Hi. What's it like out there?"

"Bloody freezing. And the snow's pitching."

"Excellent. Perhaps I won't be able to get to work in the morning."

"Possible. Have you eaten?"

"No. I was waiting for you. Fancy pasta?"

"Sounds good to me. Thanks. If you're thinking of doing it now I'll come and help, or at least sit with you in the kitchen."

"OK. Won't be long. You can sit while I cook."

Ten minutes later I was sat at the kitchen table while steam rattled from pans and Sally busied herself. I told her about what had happened during the day, and how I had taken Cernunnos around the grounds, seeking his protection. She looked a little bemused but, fair play to her, she made no criticism or negative comments.

"I hope it works," she said. "Jane is sure they've lost birds in the last few days. Oh, she told you didn't she. You said she'd phoned. And I saw a fox up the road the other day. I forgot to tell you."

"I believe it'll work. Trouble is, how can we be sure? The sign of success is that nothing happens. The birds stay safe. We can only tell if it hasn't worked, not if it has."

"Maybe if others, like Jane, are being foxed, and we're not, then that's a good sign."

"True. We'll see. It'll be interesting to see after the snow. What tracks there are."

"I never thought of that. I know there's a fox run beside the paddock fence. In the Big Meadow. We've seen fox prints there in the past. And they come through the fence up by the stream; it seems sheltered under the trees there. If the snow settles properly we may yet see. Anyway, dinner'll be ready now in a minute. In here or in front of the TV?"

Later that evening I stood in the Family Room at the patio doors. I turned on the outside light and took in the scene beyond. The snow was still falling and the world beyond the doors was predominantly white and cut-glass crystalline and sparkling. Feathery flakes tumbled past the light and their predecessors had heaped on top of the fencing, the gate, the trees, and lay peacefully on the ground. I was tempted to go for a walk round the outside of the cottage, but resisted. It would have been a shame to despoil the freshness and the virginity.

In the night we heard the foxes. The barking was unmistakable. But with the snow changing the acoustics, it was hard to tell where the foxes were. They could have been close; they could have been far. The birds heard them too, for we could also hear the fluttering panic and shuffling around in the sheds; the ducks squawked and spluttered; the cockerels crowed and the hens fussed and shouted. I asked Sally if I should go out and investigate but she just grunted, "Nothing you can do. So, no." And she, too, shuffled and snuffled and went back to sleep.

By morning time the cats had ensconced themselves on the bed and were curled up, dozing. The dawn chorus was dominated by the distinctly un-songlike noise of the crows and rooks, tempered with the two cockerels who seemed in continuous competition with each other. One would crow. You could count to five, then the other would crow. Count to five, and the first would crow, and so it went on.

As I raised myself into consciousness I recalled the snow and Cernunnos. And the foxes in the night. Sally's alarm howled and I watched as an arm sneaked out from under the duvet, pressed the snooze button, and shot back in – like a spider seizing its prey and then retreating to the edge of its web. I did not have to get up: it was school holiday time. But under the circumstances I couldn't lie there any longer. I got up and sneaked a look outside through the bedroom curtains. Brilliant! About four inches of snow. And everywhere calm, still and apparently undisturbed. Certainly no sign of death: blood and feathers usually, in the paddock.

Ten minutes later I was showered and dressed and in the kitchen with the kettle in hand. Sally padded down the corridor and went into the bathroom. I heard the shower switched on so left the kettle on and opened the back door.

It was cold but dry. The snow made satisfying scrunching noises underfoot as my wellies squashed footprints along the driveway. There were several tyre tracks in the snow on the road, so vehicles were on the move. But it wasn't vehicles I was interested in.

I went into the paddock. The guinea fowl were still in their tree; I could see them moving about in the depths of the branches. Otherwise it remained still. Snow always seems to slow the world down. It's like a heaviness has descended: paradoxical when snow is white and light.

There were no tracks anywhere in the paddock that I could see. The goats had had more sense than to venture out. They never liked the rain, let alone snow. There was plenty of hay and shelter, and two buckets of drinking water, in their shed. I would put their feed buckets in their shed later, save them having to venture out.

I walked the boundary, trying to exactly retrace my steps from the previous evening. There was nothing. Not a track in sight. Not even prints from the wild birds. Of course, the foxes may have been elsewhere. Or the snow may have covered tracks after they had been around. As I had said to Sally: success would be nothing happening.

I crossed the stream and headed under the washing line. The bathroom window was steamed up and I could make out Sally's shape. The last chance to find anything would be where the stream came down the mountain. But there was a possibility that sheep and lambs had come up to the fence: Padraig was keeping a flock in the Big Meadow and they had access to the stream banks above the cottage.

I couldn't see any sheep or lambs in the Meadow. They may have been taken inside during the evening. Anyway, I went up to the fence. I leaned over to look. It was difficult to make out anything; the brambles and nettles were weighed over with snow, and fallen branches protruded like the bodies of soldiers killed in no-man's land.

There was nothing for it: I had to climb over the fence and walk up through the copse and check very carefully. So I did. And I found footprints. Just like a dog they were. Perhaps they were a dog? One set of prints that came down the mountain from the direction that I had gone in when out with the shotgun. The direction that pointed towards the fox lair.

I sidestepped the tracks so I could follow them without covering them. Sometimes, when they went through scrub and thicket that was too dense I had to scout around, but eventually I was able to trace them all the way to where I had seen the dog fox. Now I turned around and headed back to the cottage. I was rather excited and tripped and stumbled at times. About 50 yards before the fence I slowed down. Very carefully I noted where the tracks were. And where they stopped. Because they did stop. They stopped a few yards away from the fence, and then headed off at a sharp angle. The fox had been heading straight for us, and at the last minute had turned away. There was no doubt. It was there. I had the evidence!

I followed the newly discovered set of prints for a while. They crossed Jimmy's garden and seemed to then head off across the road. Maybe later I'd walk up the road to see if I could find them.

I stood under one of the ash trees and closed my eyes. In some ways I felt too excited, but I knew I had to send out my thanks to Cernunnos/Herne and his hounds. So that's what I did. As I was doing so the back door opened and Sally came out.

"Is it too deep for me to get to work?"

"Probably not. The fox was here. But stopped at the fence. It worked! Last night. It worked!"

"Oh excellent. I'm just going to phone Michael to see what it's like in the village. Then maybe Lisa to see if the town's clear and if anyone else is going to work. OK?"

"Yeah. Right. OK."

I felt deflated. She was not dismissive but neither did she share my sense of... triumph, I suppose it was. Yet I still was able to feel excited. This was an important lesson to me. What it taught me was to be circumspect about my spiritual experiences. I knew that we had stopped the foxes, Herne and I. I knew that without his intervention Sally might now be picking up carcasses and searching hedges and trees for hens and ducks that might have escaped. That she could be flinging headless birds into Padraig's hedges down the road. That she would be counting the cost of losing dozens of birds. I also knew that this was essentially a personal and private experience: not one to shout about, but one to quietly celebrate internally. I wanted to share this with somebody I cared about; but it was obvious that I could not. And perhaps should not. Not for now anyway.

And that was the most important thing. I knew. I knew it was real. And I knew that I could maintain this protection and that, ultimately, I could prove nothing. But then, I had proved everything I needed to prove, and proved it to myself. This was a glorious feeling.

I kicked the snow. I picked it up and threw it at the trees opposite. I kicked again. Like a child let loose among piles of autumn leaves. Then I turned back towards the paddock and went to open the shed. The sun was shining, the world was white and sparkling. It was time to give the birds their morning feed.

Chapter Two

One of the regular late spring or early summer jobs is to keep the grass under control in the paddock. The paddock is about the size of a football pitch but slopes down from stream to road. It is more reminiscent of an ancient burial mound with plenty of folds rather than a decent sports playing surface.

However, it can be cut with a fairly heavy-duty petrol mower. Once I had a go with a scythe. Daft idea. The scythe was good on the nettles along the ditch, the roadside verges, but on paddock grass it was worse than useless. Or perhaps it was me that was worse than useless. Something happened: I don't know whether it was that I hit bumps in the ground too often or that my swing was too violent; but the evening after I had envisaged myself as a 'man of the country' sweeping away the grass with traditional tools (not quite saying "oo arh oo arh" as I went), I discovered I had knackered my shoulder. Well, at least I hadn't chopped off my leg. In the morning I was in agony.

So that afternoon I took myself off to the doctors. This was the first time I had been to a doctor in Ireland. It costs money. Anyway, my doctor (that is, Sally's doctor) has a surgery in Avoca. For those who watch *Ballykissangel* on television, Avoca is the real place where it is filmed. The surgery is in a hut on the hill – midway between the pub, Fitzgeralds, and the church, but on the opposite side of the street.

It's a 'first come first served' set up. There is no receptionist to quiz, comfort or annoy you: just a small waiting area with about ten chairs arranged around the walls. The 'surgery' is a small room off one end of the hut. The doctor arrives (usually half an hour late), gives a cheery public greeting to all waiting, goes into his surgery and then a couple of minutes later pops out with a small and tinny portable radio. He plugs this in by the door, turns it on and disappears into his room. Next time he appears it is to ask for the first patient.

When it is my turn we make our introductions. I tell him why I am there and why I chose him. He remembers Sally clearly, she has been seriously ill in the past: this is one of the reasons I came to Ireland. Social niceties completed, he decides to give me a cortisone injection and advice. I accept both. He then, almost apologetically, asks me for €30, and if that is OK. I assure him it is and hand over the cash. I gather from listening to pub talk that he is a fair doctor, and his charges vary considerably, according to patients' circumstances.

So now I use the mower to cut the grass. I first take on the lawn at the front. No problem. I could then attack the side of the cottage: "the grassy bank" as we call it – the patch outside the patio doors or the strip under the clothesline. I do none of these. I tackle the paddock. This is not in order to keep down the paddock grass; ultimately the livestock could eventually manage this. It is for two reasons. The first is that cutting the grass encourages fresh growth and takes out the wild mint and the weeds. But the main reason is that if the grass gets too long, the hens and ducks find it more difficult to move around. So, I have taken to cutting poultry paths. I create tracks, several feet wide, where the grass is shorter. The tracks run from the bird sheds to the feed troughs; from the centre of the paddock to the stream, and from wherever I feel like it, to... well, wherever I feel like it.

Sweetie doesn't like the petrol mower, but Circe is quietly interested. The first few occasions I passed by her in the paddock she pretended to charge at the mower. When this had no effect she sidled up to it, as I was pushing, and walked or trotted alongside. But now this is a boring game so usually she ignores us.

I had just finished my first poultry paths of the season and had turned off the mower. I heard Circe bleating. She is not, by nature, a very voluble goat. Of course, when she's in season she makes a racket all night (and a goat in season is said to "be calling": a good euphemism) but mostly she only makes a noise when disturbed. So now I looked around. I could not see her, nor her mother. I traced the bleating to behind the duck shed. And discovered Circe standing alongside Sweetie, who was lying on her side and kicking her legs.

Even a skinny, old, dowager goat is not a lightweight, especially when you have an injured shoulder. Nevertheless, I wrapped my arms around Sweetie and lifted her to her feet. Slightly unsteady, but managing to stay upright, she wandered off as if nothing was wrong and began nibbling at hawthorn in the hedge. This was a good sign: she was still interested in food. Goats are browsers, not grazers, but even Sweetie's teeth, and presumably gums, were up to snacking on leaves and twigs.

Still, it seemed to be only a matter of time before Sweetie died. Or had to be put down. The practical implications of this also had to be considered. Circe needed to have a companion. With her mother gone, we would need another goat. And what better than Circe's kids? It was time to think again of Circe being mated.

While there might be a widespread and accessible poultry keepers' community around us, the same cannot be said for goatkeepers. There were wild goats on the mountainside at Glencummin; there was a goat farm on the way to Dublin, but Sally did not know of any potential impregnators for Circe.

That evening we discussed what to do. Sally got on the phone to try to tap into the network of people who might know. Unfortunately the billy that Circe had mated with before was no more, and nobody knew of a possible alternative.

Michael, who lives in a tin-roofed shack under a waterfall in Glencummin, did tell Sally that the wild goats on the mountain were close by to him. There was, of course, no guarantee that next time Circe was calling they'd still be there, but as she was due in a couple of days there was a distinct chance. And Michael was sure that the small herd of goats had a wild billy among them. So that was a possibility.

The goat farm phone number was not working, so we gave that up as a bad job. It looked as if it'd have to be the mountain.

Saturday arrived. It was a bit of a 'soft day': drizzly, but good enough to take Circe across to Michael. She had been calling since Thursday night, and wagging her short, stumpy tail, so was obviously in season. Usually on a Saturday we would take the duck eggs to Ballydrum where the local butcher would buy them from us and put them on sale in his shop. However, today would have to be goat-mating day.

The plan was to put Circe in the trailer and drive the few miles to Glencummin. We would put her on a long tether in one of the fields above Michael's cottage and pick her up again on Sunday evening. If we didn't tether her she may well disappear with the wild goats and, although she'd eventually return, we couldn't expect Michael to take the responsibility.

For the first part all went according to the plan. Sally phoned Michael who confirmed the goats were a few hundred yards up the mountainside, and that he would be in all morning.

Circe quite likes travelling in the open trailer. It appeals to her curiosity. So we put straw on the base and walked her in. We secured her: a goat trying to leap out of a trailer at 30 mph is not a good idea, and set off.

Wicklow lanes, like most Irish roads, are renowned for their potholes. It was, therefore, a bit of a bumpy ride for Circe. The winter rains scour out chunks of road surface. The local authority sends out three men and a lorry. The men fill the holes with gravel and, if you're lucky, stick a bit of tar on the top. The next day it rains again and the 'repair' is washed away. Still, it keeps men in work.

Getting to Michael's cottage is, at the best of times, a mini-adventure. We are on the road that leads past his home. Parking the car on the road is inadvisable; it is rather narrow. But the rocky track from the road is steep and has a sharp bend. At the end of the short track there is just enough room to make a 7-point turn. But with a trailer attached this is impossible. So we disconnect the trailer from the car, leave it on the roadside and Sally drives extremely cautiously down the track, parks and we come back for the trailer. However, with Circe in the trailer it will be madness to try to manoeuvre it. Sally takes Circe out and I take the trailer and leave it in next door's farmyard.

Once we have Circe at the bottom of the track we have to all ford the river to get to Michael's land. There are large stepping stones across the river, but Circe is strong and nervous. It doesn't help that Michael keeps geese. While they may look graceful and serene on the water, as soon as they see us arriving they swim to the land and start honking and hissing. So I take Circe and leave the geese to Sally. Or Sally to the geese.

Circe is sure-footed; I am not. It is fortunate that the river is shallow at the moment and, being a gentleman, I let our lady goat walk across the stones while I let my wellies take the strain in the water. We both make it safely across but my heart is pounding and my arms stretched because Circe has wanted to cross the river somewhat faster than I.

While we were crossing, Sally and Michael had marshalled the geese into their shed. Although Circe is accustomed to poultry, geese are more intimidating than hens and ducks. I suspect that if she were not in season we would not have got her to attempt the stepping stones. All I want to do now is rest; all Circe wants to do is run off.

I wrap Circe's tether around a tree and secure it. She bleats and calls. I have a chat with Michael and Sally.

After a few minutes, during which Michael points up the mountain to some scrubby bushes, we spot a small herd of wild goats in the distance. They are all horned. Circe is not. This could be a problem; they could injure Circe. Also, Michael has made the assumption that one goat with particularly spectacular horns is male. This may not be the case. It could be that the whole herd is female. We are not close enough to see. Or to smell. The male of the species can be detected by smell from quite far off.

All we can do is try. Circe seems keen enough to venture up the mountain but both Sally and I are nervous. I suppose we feel protective towards our Circe. It feels like we are the parents of a sensitive child who is about to be let loose into the hurly-burly of a school playground for the first time. But we have come this far; and Circe is ready for mating. We have to go for it.

Michael has thoughtfully already taken a bucket of water and a bucket of feed up into a field that overlooks his cottage. So now it is just a question of taking Circe along sheep paths, through several gates, and finding a suitable tethering point. We are pretty sure that the wild goats are watching us. They only have one direction of 'escape'; they obviously will not come in our direction; to our left is the waterfall that tumbles all the way from the top of the mountain, past Michael's cottage and into the river; to their right the stone walls seem solid and impenetrable: brambles cover any gateways. So the only way for them is up. As it is for us.

Circe leads the way with some urgency. Perhaps she can scent a billy. She bleats, pricks her ears and wags her tail. All encouraging signs.

After about 15 minutes of climbing and negotiating various natural obstacles, we arrive at what seems a good place. It is within sight of Michael's, so he can keep an eye open; it is reasonably sheltered with trees and bushes, should it rain; it seems to have access for the wild goats and one of the trees is sturdy enough to take Circe's tether.

I tie Circe to the tree and show her the buckets. She is not interested. All she does is bleat and strain at the end of the rope. Sally is still unsure of all of this. After some debate she heads back down the mountain and returns soon with two feedbags. In one there is straw, which she proceeds to scatter under the tree so that Circe can have comfortable bedding (unlike the wild goats, which seem to manage perfectly well without), and in the other is fresh hay. This she piles at the base of the tree in case Circe wants a snack during the night.

Somewhat reluctantly we all say our farewells to Circe. Of course, Michael and I make rather coarse remarks full of unsubtle innuendo, while Sally keeps turning to check that her pet is OK. Circe is watching us go, but seems unperturbed.

That evening the paddock is strangely quiet once the birds have been put to bed. No Circe calling; just Sweetie in the goat shed, leaning heavily against the wooden walls, lifting a front leg now and again, obviously in pain. She sways from side to side and rubs her skinny body along the timbers, scratching. We will soon be faced with the dilemma that all animal owners and keepers have eventually: do we let her live on in pain, or do we put her out of her misery? Not that she seems miserable. Maybe she's stoical. How can you tell? She's eating as normal; but she continues to lose weight and definitely seems to be in pain at times.

Sally seems tempted to phone Michael to check on Circe, but knows that is pointless. Eircom have no telephone landlines to Michael's cottage: so the only phone they have is a mobile. Because of the mountains around it is easier for Michael to phone out than it is for us to contact him. If he wants to phone then he has to either cross the ford – and after a few drinks and at the dead of night this is not recommended, and then stand in the road; or he has to perch on a stone boundary wall near the waterfall, on tiptoe, with his head among the branches of one of the ash trees. So no phoning tonight.

The evening is proving to be quite pleasant. The drizzle has gone, leaving a humid but warm feel to the air. The clouds still cover the sky. No stunning sunset to gawp at tonight; and the wind has dropped completely. It is tempting to sit outside the Family Room, on the bench that looks out over the paddock.

I get a cloth and wipe the damp, and chicken droppings, from the bench. Hens have no problem invading our space; indeed, if we leave the patio doors open in high summer it is not unknown to find a couple of birds wandering happily around the Family Room. Mind you, I've even found Circe doing the same. Fortunately the sounds of her hooves give her away; just as well because she'd eat the house plants and the newspapers that lie scattered around. Not to mention the library books.

So I sit outside, slightly chilly but warm enough in sweater and jeans. The darkness descends and Sally comes outside to sit next to me. She has brought us both a gin and tonic.

If we turned on the outside light moths would bother us, so the only artificial light is that which is spilled from the kitchen.

As we sip our drinks the crows and rooks become silent. The lambs and sheep occasionally call across the neighbouring fields. I can imagine the lambs searching for their mothers in the dark... only able to detect them by sound.

By the time it is nearly completely dark the rapid fleeting shapes of bats skirt amongst the trees, their silhouettes just discernible against the clouds. Their high voices soon become the only focus of our attention. We feel like we are imitating the cats when they go fly-catching: our eyes dart from side to side, up and down, trying to determine exactly what it is we are seeing.

Sally reminded me of the time she rescued a bat.

One early spring afternoon she'd been in the paddock and was tidying around the sheds. Near the feed shed wall was an old bucket and in the bucket, struggling in the dirty old rainwater and rust from the handle, was a small bat. She took the bat out and brought it into the cottage. It was barely alive so she made up a cardboard box and put papers and rags in the bottom. The bat settled and remained still for several hours. When it was dark she took the bat out and placed it on the trunk of one of the trees near the road. It clung tenaciously to the bark. A few hours later, when she went back to check, it had gone.

We had also rescued a racing pigeon. It had arrived one day and slumped on the roof of the henhouses. It was exhausted. A few days of gentle nurturing, and feeding and watering, seemed to restore it. We could not decipher the ring but it was obviously used to being handled. On a couple of occasions we took it out of the shed where we'd contained it and encouraged it to fly off. One day it did. And then a friend told us that if it was a racing pigeon its owner would not be impressed with it: it would have been days late in its return, and he would probably wring its neck. But at least we had done our bit.

All this talk of rescuing brought us back to Circe. At least the weather was fine so, although she might be distressed – a huge change in routine for her, alone, on the mountainside, with the possibility of a randy billy goat close by – she would basically be fine. If this attempt at mating her didn't work we had nowhere else to try. Her next season would be in three weeks, which did give a bit more time, but what could happen in three weeks to change the availability of a billy? If it did work, then her kids (goats, like sheep, normally have twins) would be due in five months. Gestation for a goat is about 150 days.

With a big sigh, Sally took our now empty tumblers and went back indoors. I followed, closing the patio doors.

At ten on Sunday morning the phone rang. It was Michael. He was reporting that all was well. Circe was still on the mountain. The wild herd was nowhere to be seen.

Sally was tempted to fetch Circe at once, but we decided that it would do no harm to leave her. If she hadn't mated then a few more hours might help; better that than having to return every three weeks or so. Especially as today the weather was fine.

When the weather is fine you have to take advantage of it and do all the outdoor things that can't be done because it's lashing with rain. Consequently Sally and I spent most of Sunday morning in and around the paddock.

I took on the job of making paper logs. We had recently bought, via the Internet, a log-maker. We had loads of newspapers that we usually burned, either on the stove in the lounge or in the incinerator where we burned all our flammable rubbish. Recycling of paper is non-existent around here; presumably it's not a viable economic proposition.

With a proper log-maker we could be more 'green' and also save money and effort by cutting back on the wood we burned. We buy in a supply of logs every year, which we store under tarpaulins and then split with an axe as and when either we need them or the weather is good enough to be outside. We also sometimes scour neighbouring fields and the bogland for fallen branches, bowsaw in hand. Now, though, we can create our own logs.

I took out the piles of newspapers, grateful that Circe was away. One of her favourite games is to pick up the papers from where I place them on the concrete and run round the paddock with them flapping in her mouth. She pauses to check she has my attention, turns, runs, stops and looks again. The idea is to chase her. Well, that's *her* idea. It can be exhausting: sometimes fun, sometimes a distraction. Sweetie is too old for this and totally ignores what is going on: a somewhat supercilious attitude I sometimes think.

Before we can put the paper in the log-maker it has to be soaked in water. We have a large orange plastic laundry trolley that we fill with water from the hose. The sheets of newspaper are then screwed up and dunked in the trolley and left for several days. So before I can soak the present lot I have to extract the paper that's been soaking for a while.

The water is cold and the work wearing on my back. I take out soggy balls of soaking and dripping paper, and drop them in the metal box. Once the box is full, and the water is draining out of the holes in the bottom, I take hold of the two handles and push the pressure plate on to the paper. This squeezes the water out. Releasing the handles I can turn the box over and tap out a paper briquette, now ready to be dried. It can take a couple of minutes to do one paper log properly. They are stacked under another tarpaulin on wooden palettes where they dry. If I left them in the sun then Circe would either eat or destroy them, and I suspect that Sweetie would join in with this one.

While I am doing this, Sally is sweeping behind the birdhouses. Winter detritus never seems to disappear. And the birds kick dirt and stones, grass and dead leaves all over the place. This can then block the drain-holes I have created in the hedge and bank behind the sheds, and we can have a flood during a rainstorm. So good housekeeping is essential.

After an hour or so we both stop and have a cup of tea – Sally leaning against the broom, me slumped on the concrete slab next to the briquettes. The hens are pecking throughout the paddock, with the occasional apparent rape as one of the cockerels gets bored. The ducks are either in the stream or in the Big Meadow. Superficially and to the untrained eye it is a scene of rural contentment. To the trained eye it continues to be a scene full of tension and power struggles. We have too many cockerels and too many drakes. The females are having a bit of a hard time.

Sweetie also seems to be having a hard time. She is limping quite badly and seems reluctant to move at all. When she stands still she continues to raise each front leg in turn, and sways from side to side. Already today I have had to pick her up twice as she has fallen. It is fortunate that these are school holidays when I am not working, so I can be around to help her. Sally can only really be around one week in three; the other two weeks her shift pattern means that she has to spend a lot of the daytime sleeping.

As we sip our tea Sally reminisces about Sweetie. As Sally's first goat she obviously means a lot to her. And Circe is Sweetie's daughter. Sally just hopes that Sweetie will live long enough to see another batch of grandkids. Although I don't say it, I somehow doubt it. I am beginning to know things that I don't know how I know but I just know. And one of those is that Sweetie will be dead before Circe gives birth.

Where that 'knowing' comes from I have no idea. Trying to

determine which thoughts come from my Ego and which come from the Unconscious, or the Universe, is a problem I am having. As is the notion that maybe I am being too grandiose. But these things are becoming more and more a part of who I am. And it is a part that I have to be circumspect about sharing. Obviously Sally has years of experience looking after these creatures; and even accounting for possible wishful thinking on her part, I knew that I could not challenge her view. So, for now, I say nothing to disturb her.

Once I have emptied the laundry trolley of the newspapers I top up the water using the hose. Then it's scrumpling up the next batch of newspapers and throwing them in to soak. Leave for a few days and begin the process all over again.

Sally has finished the cleaning and tidying, and is now checking inside the empty bird sheds. Rats can be a problem so a regular inspection for rat runs or chewed floorboards in and around all the animal sheds is essential.

After lunch we prepare to fetch Circe back. I decide to check my emails whilst Sally is getting everything ready. In the Inbox is a message from our Internet provider. Several weeks back I had entered a Prize Draw for travel vouchers. The message says we have won! €2000 worth! I reply as requested, wondering if it's a hoax, and then I close down the computer and rush out to tell Sally.

She is not as excited as I am, concentrating on the tow hitch, but nevertheless I start making suggestions about where we could go. She asks if we can discuss this later. Feeling a little disappointed I agree, and let my 'bubbling' stay within.

On the journey to Michael's we say little. Eventually we arrive and from the road we can see Circe in the distance. It looks like she has either spotted us or heard the car; she is stretching her tether to its full length and is bleating. She wants to come home.

I sort out the trailer and Sally crosses the ford. When I get to Michael's cottage he and Sally are already climbing up the mountainside. The geese are nowhere to be seen. So I follow on up and catch them just as they are entering the field that Circe is in. She is OK, no doubt about that. Sally goes up to her and hugs her, and Michael gathers the buckets. I kick the straw and hay around the field... no point in taking it back, and leave it for the wind and rain to disperse.

Circe is no longer wagging her tail and there is a distinct whiff about her. It is almost certain that a billy has been close to her. Just how close remains to be seen. We should know for sure within the next month. If, in three weeks' time, she fails to come into season it is a sure thing she is pregnant. We should also be able to tell by her demeanour over the next few days. The chances are that if she is expecting she will go all soppy and a bit quiet.

On the way down she is submissive. This is a relief. We say quick farewells and thanks to Michael, and with little trouble take Circe across the river and put her in the trailer. The smell is even more noticeable in the shelter of the trailer.

Once home Circe allows herself to be led into the paddock, hens scattering out of her way. She goes straight into her shed and lies down.

It is only then that I see Sweetie. She has managed to cross one of the bridges across our stream but has, again, fallen. I call Sally and together we pick her up. Sweetie stands, swaying. At least she is now on a poultry path, so staggering back to her shed for the night should be easier. I ask Sally if we should call the vet, but Sally feels there is little he can do. I suspect that she is concerned about what the vet will suggest. I leave it.

Sally pulls some of the budding leaves from one of the ash trees and hand feeds Sweetie. Although the leaves are eaten, even this now seems to be a painful process.

I offer to put the birds to bed; it is starting to near dusk. Sally is happy for me to do that. First I replenish the water buckets – we have four dotted around the paddock – and turn off the hose. I then call the birds in and we play our usual game. After a few minutes all hens and ducks are counted in and safely ensconced in their sheds for the night. Sally has gone indoors so I check the goat shed. Their water bucket needs topping up too.

When I am satisfied that all is well in the paddock I head for indoors. I pause by the paddock gate and check that Herne is still 'doing his thing'. I feel that he is, so head on in.

When I get inside I can hear the telephone ringing. Sally answers so I shut the back door quietly, having left my wellies in the back porch. I have also gathered some kindling with which to light the stove.

I lay the twigs and firelighters and have to go back out to fill the coal bucket. I also collect some of the split logs and put them in the log-basket. We have no paper logs dry enough for this evening. As soon as I put a match to the fuel in the stove and close its door, Dizzy and Winston amble in and lie on the hearthrug.

I gather from the snatches of telephone conversation I overhear that Sally is talking with Stacey, her friend from New Zealand. Stacey and David had lived locally, actually on the road to Glencummin that we had driven today. They had emigrated to New Zealand a couple of years ago. Once they had been Sally's best friends.

While Sally was still chatting I go into the kitchen and put on the kettle. I make two mugs of tea, give Sally hers and wander into the lounge. The fire was blazing so I shift the cats, top up with coal and put my feet on the coffee table and lie back to sip my tea.

When Sally has finished she comes in and sits on the sofa.

"How's things?" I ask her.

"Fine," she says. "That was Stacey. They're both well."

"Good."

There's one of those awkward silences.

"Stacey wants me to visit. In their springtime. September."

"That's nice. And...?"

"And I said yes. You don't mind do you?"

"Why should I mind?"

"Well, I'd like to use the vouchers."

"Ah."

Sally puts down her mug and perches on the arm of the chair I'm sprawled in.

"This might be the only chance."

"OK."

"I'll pay you back. Make sure you have half. Because I want to, need to, go. Alone. And you'll be at school anyway."

"Right."

"And you're so good with the animals. You really don't mind?"

"No. I don't mind. But what about Circe?"

"Christ! Yes. Oh, she'll be fine. She'll be due when I'm away, won't she? But goats can do it all alone. It won't be a problem. Never has been. Last time she waited until we were all out before she gave birth. We knew she was about to deliver but she wanted to be alone. I'm sure it'll be OK. And there's always Don and Jane."

It was only a few hours ago that we knew we had travel vouchers. Already they were gone. The synchronicity was astonishing. Yet it was something I would have to get used to. Not that I was totally aware of this at the time.

Over the next few weeks life continued and we drifted along.

I got into a routine of coming home from school and checking that all was well with the birds and goats. It always was. Cernunnos was continuing to offer protection, of that I had little doubt. However, I routinely 'topped up' the boundary walk we had taken. Occasionally we would hear from neighbours of how foxes had taken poultry, sometimes decimating flocks. But ours remained untouched. Sweetie hobbled around. Sometimes I would find her on her back or side. With Sally asleep during some daylight hours I was never sure how long our old nanny goat had lain there. But Circe had not come into season again and showed all the signs of being pregnant. I tried putting my hands on her side to see if I could feel anything... either real in the physical sense, or if I could sense anything psychically. I could do neither. Circe didn't like it so I chose not to interfere.

One weekend, when both Sally and I were at home, we went into the paddock to find Sweetie down again. This time when we stood her up she fell straight back over. Sally was quite distressed. But it was she who had to make the decision. Sweetie was Sally's goat, not mine. It seemed to me that there was nothing else we could do for Sweetie. To allow her to lie, struggling, for possibly many hours while I was at work and Sally asleep, seemed unnecessarily cruel. By now Sweetie was also having trouble with her bladder. The goat shed smelled appalling and the straw on the floorboards had been soaking for weeks. Goats are naturally very clean so this added to the all round distress.

The following week Sally was on evening shift. This meant she would be back home at shortly after midnight, but would not leave for work until 3 pm. If we had to take Sweetie to the vet, this would be a good time. It also gave Sally a little more time to try to come to terms with the inevitable.

On Monday morning Sally phoned the vet. This took some courage. She also phoned Don and Jane and explained what would be happening. Sweetie would have to be buried somewhere. When Sally had been in hospital the Crownes had looked after Sweetie and Circe on their farm. It was somewhere Sweetie knew. Don promised that he'd prioritise digging a grave for Sweetie.

The vet had asked Sally to bring Sweetie in on Tuesday. Monday night was a mournful night. Fittingly the weather was awful. There was a dramatic thunderstorm, the moon was new and the night pitch-black. As I looked out through the patio doors, waiting for Sally to return at about 12.30, the sky merged with the land so nothing was discernible beyond a few yards. The rain and hail hammered on to the concrete, and bulleted against the windows. I saw the headlights from Sally's car and she drew up on the side drive: normally she parked outside the back door. I watched from the darkness of the Family Room as she opened the driver's door and pulled her coat over her head. She ran to the paddock gate, opened it, closed it behind her and rushed to the goat shed. I went into the lounge where the fire was past its best and the cats remained content on the hearth.

A few minutes later the back door opened and Sally appeared in the lounge.

"I didn't expect you to still be up," she said.

"I thought I'd wait tonight. Want a drink?"

We sat in the lounge with the light off, gin and tonic in hand. The fire glowed and spluttered, the cats dozed. With the curtains open the lightning formed the majority of the shadows, however short-lived they may have been. We sat quietly.

The next morning the storm had abated and left everywhere looking and feeling fresh and new. While the tension of the storm had abated, the tension in the cottage was greater.

Over a muted breakfast we planned the day. We would put Sweetie in the back of my car, which was a family hatchback, and Sally would sit with her. There'd just be enough room with the seats folded back. I would drive and when we had been to the vet we would take Sweetie's body straight to the Crownes.

I left Sally to her own thoughts for a while. I let out the birds and gave them their breakfast in the troughs. A scene of perfect normality. Which for them, of course, it was. Death is just a part of life to animals – they seemed to sense nothing. Circe poked her head out of the shed and bleated; but quickly she went back in again. I did not even look for Sweetie.

I got Sally's car keys and shifted her car to the back-door drive next to the grassy bank, and moved mine to where hers had been parked. I found an old blanket, released the back seats in my car and lay the blanket on the space now available. I heard the back door close and the sound of the key turn in the lock. I found the box of tissues I always kept in the car and put them on the rug.

Sally was being stoical but understandably was upset.

"I've just rung the boys," she said, referring to her two sons who lived with their father in Dublin while at college. "I told them about Sweetie."

"OK. Good idea."

"Where is she?"

"I don't know. I've not looked."

Sally went into the paddock and came out of the goat shed leading Sweetie on a tether.

"She's so thin," she said. "Look, the collar is so loose."

Each goat had her own collar but we'd not used Sweetie's for months. There had been no need. She had remained in the paddock. In that time Sweetie had shrunk and shrivelled so much. It hadn't been noticeable because it had happened over a while, but now it was very obvious.

As Sweetie limped and shuffled towards the gate, Circe once again put her head out of the shed door; this time she watched. Sally brought Sweetie to the car. She then wrapped her arms around Sweetie and cried. Sweetie stood there. Swaying.

Sally took the tether and collar off and hung them in the porch of the feed shed. I stood and waited.

Taking Sweetie by the neck Sally pulled her the few feet towards the back of my car. Sweetie offered no resistance. She seemed to know.

Sally left Sweetie and climbed into the car. This would not work. She climbed out again. We had to get the goat into the back of the car with minimum fuss and minimum stress. Sally lifted Sweetie so her front legs were off the ground.

"I can do this," she said. "I'll take the front, you take the back. We'll lay her in. I'll get into the passenger seat and clamber over, once she's in. And thank you for the blanket."

And that's what we did. We manoeuvred Sweetie into the back of the car and all she wanted to do was lie down. That in itself was a relief. The thought of her trying to stand whilst I was driving, or trying to escape, was unnerving. But she was totally compliant. Maybe she did know what was happening and had just given up the will to live.

Once Sweetie was comfortable Sally climbed over the front seats and sat with her, cradling her head on her lap. I gently closed the hatchback door and we set off.

It was a slow journey – each pothole avoided if possible, and if not possible then driven over very gently. For the first time that I could recall we did not meet any other car on the whole of the journey to the vet. About six miles.

When we arrived I drove the car carefully into the car park. I got out, leaving Sally and Sweetie in the car, and went into the building. I explained who I was and the vet, Victor, came out. He and Sally exchanged greetings and Victor took a look at Sweetie as Sally clambered out of the car.

Victor acknowledged that Sweetie was beyond help and that the best thing would be to put her down. He went back inside and Sally opened the back of the car and sat next to her old nanny goat, stroking her flank. Sweetie hardly murmured, her eyes just flickering. In spite of the journey, which must have upset her, she had controlled her bladder. This had been a concern of mine. The ammonia smell in the car, should she have peed in the car, would have been unmanageable.

Victor returned with a syringe. He decided to inject her where she lay; to get her out of the car was unnecessary and would have added to her discomfort. He also assured us that Sweetie would feel no pain, would gasp and shudder as the muscles relaxed, would not wet the car, and would slowly slip away.

And that is exactly what happened. Sweetie died in Sally's arms.

When Victor had checked that Sweetie had, indeed, died, he

and I left Sally alone and went back into the building. There I paid him €20 – less than the real cost, but what Victor insisted upon. After about ten minutes I went back to the car.

Sally was sat in the passenger seat and had shut the tailgate. She had found the box of tissues and sat there quietly. I got in, turned out of the driveway and set off for the Crownes.

During the journey Sally talked about Sweetie and the memories she had of her. She also said that she thought that another few miles in the car and Sweetie would have died anyway. She was ready to go. I listened and made what I hoped were appropriate comments and noises.

The Crownes' farm is up a long, bendy and very bumpy driveway. The car often bottomed out, even when swerving from side to side across the track in order to avoid the largest craters or biggest boulders. We drove past the cattle, past the horses and past the sheep. After a half-mile we approached the gate to the garden, which separates the farm from the domestic premises. Sort of. Really it is all part of the same property, but Jane is determined to have her square yards of lawn and flower beds.

We stopped at the gate as it was closed. Don and Jane had seen my car and were walking from the house towards us. Sally got out of the car and hugs were exchanged. I got out and walked up to Don. He told me he'd dug a grave near the cowshed because from there it was possible to see Sally's cottage. How very thoughtful!

We discussed how to get Sweetie from the car to the grave and, with Sally's agreement, we decided that Sally and I would put Sweetie in the bucket of the tractor and Don would drive her the fifty yards through the field. He would lower the bucket and he and Sally would place Sweetie in the grave. Although this might appear slightly ignominious for Sweetie, we felt sure she would not mind. Don put straw into the tractor bucket before we lifted in our dead goat. Then he slowly drove to the pile of earth that marked the spot, the rest of us walking solemnly behind.

When we got there he lowered the bucket to waist height.

Looking at the hole he had dug it was obvious he had dug it by hand. We had anticipated that he would have used the tractor. He must have sweated for at least an hour with spade and nailbar, removing soil and rocks. And, again, in the bottom of the hole he had placed straw. We were very lucky to have such good and kind friends.

Sally and Don lifted Sweetie out and gently rolled her into the grave. Jane and I stood to one side. Sally leaned into the hole and straightened out Sweetie so she was lying neatly and comfortably. Don handed her a spade and she started to fill in the dirt on top of Sweetie. Jane, Don and I stood back and gave Sally the space.

Sally finished backfilling the grave and stood up. She thanked Don and walked back across the field on her own. Jane commented upon how much Sweetie had meant to Sally and assured me that we had done the right thing. Don added that Sweetie had been surprisingly light as he lifted her off the tractor. And he was used to dealing with dead animals; every farmer has to be.

Sally declined the invitation to stay for a cup of tea, and we headed back home in silence. I parked the car and Sally went straight into the paddock and found Circe. I left them to it and went indoors. It was not yet time to light the fire, but I cleared the ashes and lay the stove ready for the evening.

When I went outside again after about twenty minutes Sally was nowhere to be seen. This was not unusual. She would sometimes go somewhere on her own without telling me. So I wandered around, checking the water buckets, chatting to the birds and Circe, and generally tidying around.

After an hour or so Sally reappeared. She had been down the road to see Lisa and her family. Lisa was the daughter-in-law of Padraig who owned the land around us. She and Pat, Padraig's eldest, had four girls: two just in secondary school, one in primary, and one due to start school in September. The girls used to help out Sally when she went away, by feeding the birds or keeping an eye on the goats. She had not told them of Sweetie's impending demise and now that the deed was done felt the urge to visit them.

The following day at work I had an idea. On my way home I called in at a local nursery to find something to plant as a memorial to Sweetie. In the end I couldn't choose so bought a weeping willow and a weeping copper beech. I had not discussed this with Sally but could not see it being a problem.

I got home after Sally had left for work and I set to planting the trees. The willow I put just above the stream near the paddock fencing. The copper beech I put on the grassy bank. I knew each tree would need protection from stray animals so built a sort of stockade of old fence posts and chicken wire around them both. It looked ugly but I did not want the trees to be eaten before they were even established. Some of Padraig's cows had been known to wander around the cottage and cows have long tongues. They could reach over and lick the trees to death! Fresh green leaves would be a great feast. Also, Circe used to escape from the paddock sometimes and wreak havoc on any attempt at growing garden plants.

I went indoors and cooked myself a meal. Sally would see the trees late tomorrow morning when she got up; but I would be at work by then. I was tired so had no intention of staying up.

After eating I put the birds to bed, checked Circe was OK, and came back in to the kitchen. There were strange noises coming from behind the cooker. They seemed to be scratching-type sounds; they weren't actually in the kitchen – I didn't think. I pulled the cooker out from the wall a little and listened carefully. The sounds were moving up and down, inside the wall.

I knew the cottage was over a hundred years old. The walls were a real mix. Some were thick stone, others were cavities filled with horsehair, dirt and rubble. Perhaps the rubble was moving around and settling. Yet the sounds were too regular. I turned off the electricity and unscrewed the cooker power point. The noise got temporarily louder and then stopped. I thought it could have been mice; but then why didn't the cats show an interest?

The cats were skilled hunters… but it wasn't usually mice they caught. Sometimes we'd get a shrew dumped just inside the catflap. At this time of year they tended to bring in baby rabbits. The worst time was when I went into the lounge early one morning and saw a glass bead on the hearthrug. Only it wasn't a glass bead. It was a rabbit eye. And then there was the time Sally looked in the bottom of her wardrobe in our bedroom and discovered the headless body of a rabbit, neatly arranged on top of some of her clothes. We never did find the head! Once a rabbit had been caught the best thing was to leave the cats to it, even if the baby bunny was alive. The squealing from the rabbit was appalling; but to wrestle the cats for it was futile.

However, there were no rabbits in the kitchen wall, of that I was fairly sure. So I supposed it must have been mice.

I put back the power point and replaced the cooker. There was nothing I could do. I'd have to hope the mice disappeared on their own. At least for now they were quiet.

I went back into the lounge and berated the cats for their uselessness. They seemed unimpressed. Both opened one eye at me, they yawned in unison and went back, presumably, to their cat dreams. So I watched TV for a while.

Next morning I got up, leaving Sally to sleep on. She had come to bed at about 1.30 am. When she got home in the early hours she usually spent some time playing FreeCell on the computer before coming to bed. Last night was no exception. I gathered my clothes from where I had left them ready, in one of the other bedrooms, and went into the bathroom. After I had finished in there I started to get my breakfast. Today I chose to have toast and honey. I found the bread and put it into the toaster. Only, when I pressed the handle to drop the bread into the toaster, the bread jammed halfway. I took the bread out and tried again. Nothing different.

I knew that Sally sometimes made herself some toast when she got in from work so assumed the toaster was jammed with crumbs. I took the bread out and peered inside. There was definitely something blocking the mechanism.

I found a screwdriver from the hall cupboard and, having unplugged the toaster and put it upside down on the kitchen table, having first put newspaper down to catch the crumbs, I unscrewed the bottom plate. In the bottom of the toaster, stuck between the elements, was the source of the problem. It was a well-toasted mouse.

I decided to skip breakfast for today. I removed the almost incinerated body from its makeshift crematorium and threw it outside on to the grassy bank. I doubted the cats liked their meat that well cooked, but a crow might. Waste not, want not. All leftover food is deposited on the grassy bank: the hens will eat most things from pasta to... yes... roast chicken. I left a note for Sally explaining what I had found. This is the way we usually communicated during the working week when she was on evenings or nights.

When I came back from work I found a note from Sally thanking me for the trees and for the information about the toasted mouse. Before she had gone to work she had carried out more repairs on the birdhouses and asked that I check them out to see if anything else needed doing. So I went and inspected as requested and found all in good shape. Sally wanted to ensure that as much as possible was done before she tripped to the other side of the world for three weeks. Her note also suggested that we meet on Friday at River Manse for a drink and a game of snooker.

River Manse is our nearest 'watering hole'. It is a newly built hotel about 10 minutes' drive from here. The guests have included many celebrities, including BBC Radio One DJs, pop stars and sporting stars. It is not unknown for some to arrive by helicopter, just for lunch. Their restaurant is superb. But I am not an advertisement for them. For us the main attraction is that they have a snooker room. Much of the hotel's trade is at weekends; they are booked all year for weddings on a Saturday. Weeknights, especially off-season, it can be quiet down there. We have got to know the staff, and owners, well. One summer vacation one of Sally's sons worked there behind the bar.

So that evening I went to their bar at about nine and waited for Sally to arrive from work. It was always interesting sitting in the lounge on one of the huge sofas. The peat fire would be glowing and the conversation around worth listening in to. There was a small scattering of guests this particular Friday so all I did was sip my Guinness and talk to the bar staff about their day and how busy they would be tomorrow. It was useful to find out the numbers and types of any wedding party; that would allow us to make a judgment about whether or not it would be worthwhile trying to get in the snooker room, and at what time, on the Saturday. The room only had one table and that was three-quarter size.

River Manse is actually more than just a hotel. They like to think of it as a small village. There are a couple of shops, a pub and riding stables. During the summer they regularly hold gymkhanas and hundreds of people attend. They also hold monthly 'Organic Food Fairs': another very popular event.

I managed to spin out my drink for half an hour. On Friday evening shifts Sally was able to get back home at about 9.30 pm. Sure enough, just as I was sauntering over to the snooker room to ensure it was free, and it was, she walked in through the hotel reception. She went into the snooker room and I went to the bar to get drinks. They knew us well enough by now to pour 'the usual' and bring it to us while we were setting up for snooker. Because we were not very good, our games were always entertaining. Flukes and disasters caused us both much amusement. It also allowed us the chance to talk. This particular evening we discussed Circe's pregnancy and Sally's impending visit to New Zealand. I did wonder what we would do if Circe had two billy kids. I knew how strong goats could be from taking Circe for walks so joked about a "goat and cart". Then Sally told me about the "Goat Harness Society" which advises on just such a thing. The thought of hitching two goats to a cart and have them take me to the hotel or pub was just too much. Potentially great fun. I decided to look up the Society on the Internet. Then, of course, I considered entering goats for one of the gymkhanas – but as Sally had potted the pink by mistake I concentrated on the game instead.

As Sally would be doing the 'egg run' tomorrow she would call in at the local farmers' cooperative and buy a mineral lick for Circe. This should ensure she had all the nutrients she required. Because we both were working it was not always possible to ensure that Circe had an adequate diet, or sufficient exercise, for a pregnant goat. It would be best if she could be allowed to browse the hedges and verges and eat a variety of plant life. All she had at home was the paddock grass, and that not only had hens running all over it, it was probably nutrient-deficient. It had never been reseeded in 15 years and could well be old and stale. If you were a goat.

Sally also had been up into the roof of the cottage and rummaged among the boxes and collections of books stored up there. She had found a guide to keeping goats, in which was a section on kidding and how to manage the whole process. We would go through this and leave it accessible, so that at least I had a text to which to refer when having to experience goat midwifery for the first time.

By now Circe was beginning to swell. And she stopped wanting to play, too. All I had to do was read the book, keep an eye on her, and check the calendar we had in the hall for her due date. It was likely that one day I would come home and find her with two suckling kids.

On Saturday morning Sally drove off with boxes of eggs and I drove off in the other direction to do the supermarket shopping. We tended to share cooking at weekends, except when her sons came to visit, when Sally cooked. We were in the habit of me cooking a Sunday lunch – often, somewhat bizarrely perhaps, a Tesco supermarket chicken.

This Sunday was to be no exception.

Sally worked out in the paddock while I stayed in the kitchen, apart from the occasional trip outside with mugs of tea. I think Sally was not only trying to get everything organised for the three weeks she wouldn't be here, but also to make the most of the few weeks she had before she left. Whilst I enjoyed pottering about outside, too, there were times when I was aware that Sally needed to be left alone to do her thing. By staying indoors, mainly in the kitchen, I was not intruding.

After we'd eaten the roast chicken and trimmings I ensured the carcass was unavailable to the cats and put it back in the oven. I did not enjoy stripping the last of the meat from the bones, so usually left it to Sally. It was a job for later that evening.

In the afternoon Sally continued doing whatever she was doing in and around the paddock. There was no way I could stay indoors any longer so I wandered off up the hill behind the cottage to investigate the course of the stream. In the summer it was easier to determine where to best place the various rocks that I moved around to form dams and channels. At the height of the winter rains the paddock used to flood. This was scary. Not only did water pour down the slopes, unless the plants that grew on and around the stream banks had been completely cleared, water would back up and then torrent down to the bird sheds. The ducks would be OK – though they didn't like it much, but on a couple of occasions we had found the chicken sheds with a foot or so of water above the floor. The hens would be safe on their perches, just, but it was not healthy. And Circe and Sweetie would also be flooded out and find it a distressing experience. So I had dug a channel from the existing stream along the grassy bank. This took the overflow before it could reach the paddock. When the water came tumbling down the hillside in winter, if I strategically placed rocks in the stream, I could divert enough water to create a second stream. This stream ran past the cottage back door, along the grassy bank and into the road. One of the summer jobs was to keep an eye on all this Heath Robinson drainage system. But it was also great fun messing about with water and rocks and dams…

So, after a productive afternoon we both came back indoors and settled down for an evening of word games: *Scrabble* and *Boggle*.

The cats came in and started fussing about near the oven. Sally decided that she'd had enough of being beaten at word games and surrendered. She went into the kitchen to feed the cats and strip the chicken from lunchtime.

Suddenly there was an "Oh my God!" from the kitchen. I dragged myself out of the armchair, and calling, "Are you OK?" went to see what was going on.

Sally stood there, at the kitchen table, with the partially stripped chicken on a plate in front of her. She waved a knife at me and said, "Look." I looked. It was the remnants of a roast chicken. "Go on, look." I looked again. Nothing had changed. It was still a dead, cooked, and rather nude chicken. "Look. Inside." So I peered closely into the cavity of what I had cooked for lunch. There, neatly snuggled up against the breastbone, was a dead mouse. Not toasted this time. But roasted. Sally and I looked at one another and sort of laughed. Well, we had to really.

Somehow one of the (now diminishing) population of mice in the kitchen had got inside the chicken before I had put it in the oven. Poor thing – I had roasted it alive inside our Sunday lunch. Another one of the joys of living in the countryside.

For those of a nervous disposition, it may be helpful to know that there are no more such mouse stories to tell.

Instead, it's time to move on to when Sally has left for New Zealand and the mixed feelings I have about what it may be like over the next three weeks. I still am very apprehensive. I don't know if this is Ego or intuition. I hope the former, but suspect the latter. Sally drove to Dublin so that the boys could have use of her car when she was away. We said our goodbyes and she wished me luck. Again, reassurances about Circe; again, I'm not so sure. However, I enjoy living here and looking after all the animals. And Don and Jane are close at hand.

I wanted to continue to do improvements around the cottage while Sally was away. There was decorating to do, which was impossible when she was here because of disturbing her sleep. So the first full day alone I cleared our bedroom and set to with the paint. I got the whole room done but that night had to sleep in the spare room because of the smell.

And so the days continued. Sally phoned to say that she'd arrived safely and we agreed to communicate by email. Nevertheless, I knew she wanted to enjoy her time away and would not welcome too much information from home. Anyway, a fair bit of the time she was over there she'd be travelling. She and Stacey would be touring.

By Day 150 Circe had still not kidded. It was Friday night and as I put the hens away I noticed that Circe was more sluggish than usual and that she was trying to get into the small hen shed. She was also pawing at the ground rather often. I could not stay up all night just in case she gave birth during darkness, so went to bed feeling excited but trying to curb any feelings of dread I might have had.

I got up early the next morning and looked out the bedroom window. Circe was still heavily pregnant and still standing outside the small henhouse. I showered, dressed and ate, and went to collect the eggs, put food in the troughs and let all the birds out. As usual the rush from the hens was like a mini-typhoon. They scampered up the paddock slopes to the troughs as if they'd not eaten for weeks. Then I let out the ducks. They, too, were raucous and delighted to be out again. I crawled into their shed and extracted the eggs.

As I crossed the paddock with a bowl full of eggs there was no sign of Circe. I passed her shed and she was not in there. I crossed in front of the small henhouse, and there she was. She had made herself a nest, having dislodged the hen perches with a sideswipe. I wanted to go in and stroke her and speak to her, but somehow felt that she would prefer to be left alone. So that's what I did. Even to my inexperienced eye it appeared that she was about to give birth. How could I stop myself from hanging around and watching?! But I knew that if she saw me then nothing would happen. I couldn't even really see into the henhouse from the cottage. I tried, but Circe was just out of view. A cunning goat!

I sat on a sofa in the Family Room with the patio doors open and meditated. I called upon Cernunnos but although he was there he just sat on his horse, static. I tried to go higher and contact healing angels. It was a bit of a struggle; but I put that down to my own feelings about what was playing out just a few yards away from me. Emptying my mind was not easy. So I stopped and grounded myself.

Resisting the temptation to wander out into the paddock I went and made myself some coffee. Then I wandered out into the paddock.

I opened the gate quietly, suddenly aware of how squeaky it usually is. All the birds were milling around away from the sheds. I could see splashes of water as ducks, hidden by the banks of the stream, washed and dipped. Hens squabbled, cockerels chased unwilling 'wives' while those fortunate enough to be apparently unattractive to randy cockerels, or content with their own company, dust-bathed or pecked at the ground.

I nonchalantly walked past the henhouse as if I had chores to do on the other side of the paddock. I managed to glance inside and saw Circe still standing there. Apparently nothing had happened. So I did an about turn and headed back indoors.

I still couldn't settle to anything indoors. I had tidied the whole cottage. I had cleaned the place from top to bottom. I had rearranged books on shelves. I suppose I could arrange them again; maybe by size, or colour of spine, or…

Several times I did my nonchalant walk thing. Several times I walked back. I tried approaching the henhouse from different directions, to see if I could get a better view. It all made no difference.

Then, at about midday I passed the henhouse and there was Circe, standing, and licking something on the floor. I had to stop and look. Even briefly. Yes!! There it was. A baby goat. Even from a few yards away I could see it was a light brown colour: just like its grandmother, Sweetie.

My heart beat faster now. Should I go closer? What about the second kid; if, as Sally and books said, they invariably have twins? Was it male or female? How long before I could get closer? Was it well? If it wasn't, was there anything I could do?

I almost literally jumped for joy, hissed, "Yes!" under my breath doing the fist thing that tennis players do after a great shot, and went to phone Jane. She was almost as excited as I was but she told me to continue to do nothing. Circe had given birth before and intervening would be unnecessary once the kid was born. She was a little surprised that there was, as yet, only the one. But it happened. Sheep sometimes had one, usually two, and sometimes even three. Which was a problem for feeding as a ewe can only feed two at once. Jane offered to come over but I said that if there was nothing to be done then I'd keep her apprised of what was happening and contact her later.

I gave Circe twenty minutes and went back. She was still licking the kid. Which was still lain on its right side. No sign of any other kid. This gave me doubts. I stayed in the paddock, out of her sight. A few minutes later I went closer to the henhouse. I looked hard at the kid. Circe stopped licking and flopped down on her belly. I crept forward. I could hear nothing from the henhouse. I could see only Circe and the brown, Sweetie-coloured baby. I went right up to the door. Circe hardly stirred, her back to me she was breathing hard. I knelt down and looked at the kid. My body flushed through with a gush of emotion as I realised that the baby was dead.

Countless shards of thoughts and feelings went through me. Shaking slightly I leaned in and picked up the lifeless body. Circe bleated but remained as she was. There was no sign of any other baby. I took the dead kid out of the henhouse. I crossed the paddock and laid the body on the grass outside the patio doors. I studied it. Well, 'it' was a 'him'. It was a dead billy. Beautiful colourings. I neatly arranged the body. Perfect in every way, except that he was bereft of life. I went in to get my camera. I took several pictures from different angles. I considered what to do with him. And all the while the ducks and the hens in the paddock behind me continued to do what they always did. The sun was still shining and the clouds still swarming across the sky.

I got a spade from the shed and dug a grave up under the trees near where the stream enters our property. It was sheltered there. The ash trees offered protection from the wind and wild flowers grew among the rocks. It was an undisturbed place. I went back to collect the body. No sign of Circe.

She had moved from the henhouse into her own shed. She lay in the corner. Slumped. I went over to her and sat next to her. I talked to her for a while, telling her how sorry I was. She looked at me only occasionally; mostly she stared vacantly. I patted her side, left and went into the cottage. I thought that I had better leave the burial until Don had seen the body. He might be able to tell what had been the problem. So I covered it over with an old feedbag and went indoors.

I phoned the Crownes. Don answered. I told him the sad story and he said that he and Jane would be over at once. I didn't argue. They arrived within ten minutes. Immediately Don went into the paddock while Jane and I went to look at the dead body. She could see nothing obviously wrong so I covered him over and we joined Don.

He had led Circe out of the shed and was examining her. Because there was no twin he was concerned that there was still a dead kid inside Circe. He put his hand inside her but found nothing. As he went into the cottage to wash his hands and arm Jane told me that I'd have to milk Circe. Her udders were naturally full, and with no kids to feed from her there was a danger she'd get milk fever. So Jane showed me how to do this. I then tried myself but with minimal success. After a few minutes' training I finally got the hang of it. Circe was brilliant. Just as well, I'd have to do this twice a day for a few weeks.

Don reappeared and asked me all sorts of questions. I answered as best I could but everything was a bit of a foggy whirl. He listed a whole range of possibilities and he and Jane assured me that there was nothing I had done wrong, or omitted to do. "These things happen." It was some consolation but I was still very worried about Circe: she didn't seem at all well to me, although I couldn't be specific about this. And then there was Sally. I had to tell her somehow.

After giving me some advice on what to keep an eye open for with Circe, Don and Jane left. They said there'd be no need to call the vet, unless Circe deteriorated.

Circe quietly made her way back to her shed and I went into the henhouse to replace the straw. When I had done this I had to deal with the dead baby.

I placed the body, I didn't give him a name, into the ground and took another picture. I covered him over and ensured that the last turf contained some of the wild plants. I stood there for a few seconds, pondering upon many things.

Then it was time to check on Circe again.

She lay curled up, her ears down and floppy: never a good sign. Goats can get depressed so I assumed that this was the problem. I filled her bucket with warm water and put some salt in it. She showed no interest in what I was doing – again not a good sign – and no interest in the water. Hoping that Nature was in charge and that time would, indeed, be a healer, I busied myself with unnecessary chores around the paddock.

By now dusk was approaching. I gave the birds their afternoon food somewhat later than usual and checked on Circe again. She hadn't moved. She lay there slumped. Her breathing seemed faster and uneven.

I phoned the Crownes again. They told me not to worry, that I'd done all I could. They offered to come over again, but I told them they'd done plenty already and that just knowing I could ring them was a help. Don also gently prepared me for the fact that Circe might die. This was not what I wanted to hear. He talked of septicaemia and post-traumatic stress and haemorrhage and other things that I could not take in.

I returned outside and put the birds to bed. I don't know if it was my imagination, but this evening they all went in with less fuss than ever before; even the hens going into the shed where there was now fresh straw.

Circe was getting worse. Not only was her breathing bad, she was shivering. And her eyes were starting to roll.

Again I phoned the Crownes. Jane sensibly suggested I put a rug over Circe and tried to get her to drink.

I found an old blanket and took it outside. I placed it over Circe who made no reaction at all. I took the bucket over to her but she ignored it. The feelings of helplessness I had were almost overpowering. The chances of getting the vet to come out now were slim. I had to see Circe through this myself.

I sat there, talking to her and gently stroking her side through the blanket. Occasionally she would look at me, but mostly she seemed in a world of her own.

After about thirty minutes it was getting pretty dark. I decided that I had to try the vet. I had to do something, and that I'd try to give Circe some healing myself.

I phoned the vet but there was no reply, either from the surgery number or from the mobile number left on their answer machine. So, I certainly was on my own.

I went into the Family Room and sat on the sofa, preparing to meditate. As I drifted off to... I have no idea where... I felt the energy change. This was good. I asked for help from whomever, whatever could help me give healing to Circe. It felt right to sit there and direct the healing from the cottage. So I did. But then the energies disappeared. Suddenly there was nothing. Was this inadequacy on my part? Was I doing something wrong? Was my Ego getting in the way: all my fears and anxieties? I had no idea. Then I heard an internal voice say, "We can't let you do this."

So I did what any self-respecting 50 year old would do. I phoned my mother.

She lives in Devon and has experience as a trained healer. She is part of a small healing group on the edge of Dartmoor and has given healing to many people. She should be able to advise, even if she'd no experience of goats. Anyway, I wanted to tell her what had happened.

She was obviously upset to hear my account of the day. We then had a discussion about the healing.

In the past, when she and I have had conversations on esoteric matters, I have found that while we talked my awareness of such things has increased; or at least become more apparent. Today was no exception. We talked of all sorts of possibilities and then I had a realisation. I had never sent healing to animals before; and absent healing for animals might well be different to absent healing for people, which I had done before. What I had been doing, sat on the sofa a few minutes earlier, was sending healing to *all* goats. Not just to Circe. Humans have Egos, animals have much more of a collective consciousness. Hence how herds and flocks can behave 'as one'. Hence how our baby chicks could find their way to the food troughs without any adult birds showing them. They inherit certain 'knowledge'.

So there was no way that I had the ability, or permissions, to sit in the cottage and send absent healing to Circe. Not yet. First I had to channel the energy to her, and only her, and I had to do this by being right next to her. Maybe after having sent specific energy to a specific goat I could later send her absent healing. But that was something for the future.

I thanked my mother, hung up and, taking a torch, ventured into the paddock to see Circe again.

It was with feelings of some trepidation that I went into the goat shed. There was no apparent change. The blanket was still where I had left it over her body; completely undisturbed. Circe was still breathing in a strange way, shivering and her eyes, if anything, were rolling more.

I placed the torch on a wooden pallet that we had left in the shed as a barrier between living quarters and the hay rack. Quite often during the day there's a couple of hens sat on the pallet. If the nest boxes in their shed were crowded they'd come into the goat shed and lay in the hay rack.

But now it was just Circe and I.

I settled down next to her and tried to make myself comfortable. Once I had found a position in which I thought I could sit for a while I closed my eyes, took a deep breath, and went back into meditation.

Very quickly I found myself where I wanted to be; and the energy was back. Grasping the energy I put my hands close to Circe's flank. She turned her head, but was otherwise unimpressed. I sat there for a few minutes. I moved my hands across her back. I moved my hands where I could, pausing as and when the mood took me. She sighed now and then. I could feel tingling and warmth in my palms and fingers but wasn't sure of its origins.

The light in the shed was adequate, but soon the torch dimmed. I turned it off, giving myself the opportunity to adjust from sitting to kneeling. I continued by moonlight to move my hands over Circe. She was not getting any worse, but whether or not she was getting better I had no clue.

I stayed there for about three hours. All the while Circe rested.

Eventually I felt I had to stop. I didn't feel as tired as I thought I might have, but there's a limit to everything. I told Circe what I was doing and she leaned her head back and gently nipped me. This was an excellent sign. She only ever did this before when we'd been playing. Her eyes seemed steadier now. But I could be sure of nothing.

Before leaving I asked for help for her. I'll never know if it was my imagination or not, but in the corner of the shed above where she was lying I saw a shape. It may have been a trick of the light. But just for the briefest of moments a tiny figure seemed to hover, like a Tinker Bell in the darkness. I smiled. I said my thanks. I hugged Circe's neck, picked up the torch and went out into the night.

The hens clucked a little as I passed their shed, otherwise all was calm. My legs were stiff, but I should worry! At least Circe was still alive. What her condition would be in the morning I didn't dare think. But now I knew I really had done all I could.

Once indoors I phoned Sally. David answered. It was morning over there and Sally and Stacey had just left for the day. I told David what had happened, apart from the previous immediate few hours and he assured me he'd tell Sally. Then I went to bed and slept deeply.

The next morning I half expected a phone call from New Zealand so awoke quite early. I lay in bed, reflecting on the events of the day before. I closed my eyes and tried to send Circe absent healing. It felt better this time. I was also reminded of the figure in the shed. I had forgotten about that until then. I put my trust in whatever was going on.

At about seven I got up, dressed and went straight to Circe. She was still alive. Indeed, she was standing. Some of the water in her bucket had gone. However, it was obvious she was still ill. I carried out the normal routine with all the birds, rather earlier than usual, and prepared a feed bucket for Circe. Before I let out the birds I left her bucket in the shed. If I did her bucket *after* letting out the birds then she'd have been hassled by hens wanting to dive in to her feed rather than cross the paddock to their own troughs. But Circe was not especially interested. Nevertheless I left her bucket in her shed. She might even enjoy the company of birds this morning.

I let out hens and ducks and mooched around once I'd collected eggs. Circe remained in her shed, but also remained on her feet. Her breathing was better and her eyes were back to normal. No sign of shivering either. But it appeared that overnight her usually glossy coat had lost its lustre and now she looked tatty and sad.

I had breakfast and kept calling the vet. Eventually I got through and Victor said he'd come at once.

I went back out and very amateurishly I milked Circe. I managed to get a half-bowlful in total. It should have been twice as much. Still, I was winning.

Not knowing what to do with the milk, I don't drink milk of any sort, I threw it away into the hedge. Taking the eggs I went indoors. I washed the eggs and packed them away, ready for sale, and phoned the Crownes.

I did not tell them of my healing attempts, but I did say that Victor would be over soon. Don wanted to be here when he arrived so he rang off.

Don and Victor arrived at the same time. They knew one another well. Victor inspected Circe thoroughly, and he and Don went off in a huddle and talked tactics. It was all gobbledegook to me. Eventually they seemed to come to a conclusion.

Circe was improving. Why they didn't know. Don told me that when he'd left he really thought she wouldn't make it through the night. However, she had, so now they had to concentrate on convalescence. She would be deficient in minerals and various elements and would also benefit from antibiotics. Victor would give her a jab containing the necessary tonic and the first dose of antibiotic, but I would have to finish the course, injecting her myself. Scary. This was all supposed to be a quite natural birth and aftermath, so Sally had said. Don was used to vaccinating his animals and his attitude was that it was no problem; I could do it easily. But then I was basically a city boy: or at best an urbanite. Victor showed me what to do, but I couldn't practise because the next jab was not due until this evening. When I'd be on my own. I couldn't really ask Don to keep coming over, and couldn't pay the vet to arrive twice a day just to stick a needle in a goat. So I had no choice.

Victor left the vials and instructions. He charged me a small amount and said to call him if I was worried about Circe's progress. But he said it in a way that actually meant that I shouldn't bother him unless absolutely necessary. Fair enough. He had plenty of work with 'proper' animals, I suppose. He then left.

Don and I went into the cottage and I made us some tea.

The conversation was typical Don: the parlous state of farming in Ireland, England, the world... But he was always entertaining company, and would often slip in highly amusing anecdotes. Which I always instantly forgot. Until he'd use them again. And the next time.

Then he, too, left.

I sat at the kitchen table, having waved him off, and stared at the vials, the sterilised needles, and the hypodermic... This was not what I had been expecting at all. But I had to be up to the job. There was no escape. The responsibility was now only mine. I had relished the fun parts of living here, of looking after the animals. I had dealt with the deaths of several birds. I was becoming part of the country way of life. Yet somehow this was a baptism of fire. Circe was precious to Sally. Sally had entrusted her care to me. I loved Circe. And when Sally returned there would not only be no baby goats playing in the paddock, there would not only be no Sweetie: there might also be no Circe. It was all up to me now.

I read the instructions on the leaflet. There was no getting away from it. I picked up the drugs and tapped the vial. I looked at the syringe and checked out the measurements on its side. I could do this.

That afternoon I sat in the Family Room and sent healing to Circe. When I stood up afterwards to stretch my legs I looked out through the patio doors. There she was. Standing in the entrance of her shed. I watched. She turned and went back in.

Later I put the birds away. I didn't want them around as a distraction. Once done, I took the syringe and inserted a needle. I pushed the needle into the vial and drew up the required amount. Putting the vial down on a pallet next to the feed shed I held the syringe up and tapped out the air. All well and good. That was the easy part.

Feeling like a guerrilla soldier I stealthily walked to the goat shed. Circe must have heard me coming; suddenly she was there, her head poking out. I casually walked up to her. She stayed where she was. I patted her head and scratched behind her ears. She always liked that. I gave her healing as I stood there. She hung her head and let me work my fingers around her ears. When I felt ready, when I thought we were both relaxed, I lifted my other hand and stuck the syringe into her.

I managed to quickly push the liquid in. But as soon as I had, and before I could extract the needle, Circe bolted.

She ran across the paddock. She ran in circles. And I ran after her. It was a mixture of panic and relief. She panicked and I was panicked; but I felt great relief. It must have been reminiscent of a cartoon: Circe running in circles with a syringe hanging from her flank, with me chasing after her wondering what would happen if the needle broke off. It didn't. I caught her. I hugged her. I took out the needle and led her back to her shed. Inside the shed she looked at me, looked at her feed bucket, now spilled over and went to curl up in the corner. I righted her bucket and went to refill it.

When I went back in to the shed I replaced her bucket. Suddenly a splintery shaft of the evening sunlight caught my eye. Right above where Circe lay, right above where she lay last night, right by where I had felt there was a tiny figure, there was a crack in the wall of the shed. And shining through that crack, casting its light on the opposite wall, the setting sun seemed to be sending us a gift. It was then that I realised that the tiny beam of light was shining on the spot where Sweetie used to sleep.

Chapter Three

A few months after I had worked with Cernunnos, and set up protection around the cottage for the birds, all our neighbours lost scores of hens within about a week. We had three of them – Cornelius, Jimmy and Padraig C – knocking on our door and asking if we had replacements that they could buy. Fortunately our stock was well into breeding by then. We had four broody hens, each of which hatched more than half a dozen, and a broody duck which hatched eight. One clutch of hen eggs proved to be a mix of half-bantams and full-size hens, but beggars can't be choosers: so the neighbours were all accommodated to some degree. Nobody asked why it was that we had not been foxed.

By now I had been made redundant. The Irish government had pulled the plug on the money that was used to try to keep vulnerable children in school, which is what I had been doing. So I now had time on my hands.

Where better to be redundant than Wicklow? The money was a problem, but we would manage. As it was also now school holiday time I felt I could justify having time to 'be' rather than always having to 'do'.

Nevertheless I wanted to keep usefully occupied. I asked Don if I could help him, unpaid, on his farm. Although it is essentially a one-man operation my involvement would take some of the burdens off of him. So I started going across to the Crownes on a casual basis.

One morning when I arrived Jane was distraught. She had lost many birds to a fox. We sat in their kitchen, drinking early morning tea at the table, which is always covered in papers, animal medications, syringes and the various detritus from a working farm, and chatted. She told me that Don had resorted to setting traps for the foxes. He had laid several around the farm, although he didn't want to; they were cruel, he felt he had no choice. I told her about Herne/Cernunnos and what we had done together. I suggested she do the same.

Jane was completely acceptant of my story, but felt that she would rather I carried out the ritual. This was down to her lack of confidence rather than any doubts about its efficacy. But it presented me with a logistical problem.

The Crownes had acres of land. It would take hours to walk the boundaries, which is what I had done easily at the cottage. Also, they had foxes already living on their land (if we accept the concept of land belonging to people!). I could not see us being able to remove the foxes; they would starve. There was plenty of other food... such as rabbits and smaller furry, and not so furry, creatures... for the foxes to eat. How to protect the birds and yet allow the foxes the freedom of their own habitat and to live their own lives...

I also felt less in touch with the acres of farmland than I had with the smallholding that Sally owned. There was so much more to visualise and tune into. I was not sure that I could work with Cernunnos to summon the energy, the power, the... whatever... to protect it all. Because the foxes could also attack new lambs in the fields. I knew it was not my power, but I had to be instrumental in setting it up.

I promised Jane I would try. Later.

That evening I meditated at home. When I had finished I felt that the first thing I needed to do was dowse around the Crowne farmhouse to familiarise myself with the location. Their birdhouses were all quite close to the farmhouse, even if the birds themselves did wander away. But I had no dowsing tools, no rods or pendulum.

I let myself be guided and knew that I could make rods myself. There was no need to cut hazel twigs or any other wood. All I required was something that would indicate certain energies. So I found a wire coat hanger and untwisted it. I then cut it in two, straightened the pieces and there were my dowsing rods.

I have already talked briefly of synchronicity.

Just as I had completed making my rods Don phoned. He said his septic tank was flooding the garden and would I be across in the morning. If so, was I prepared to help him find the blockage and repair the damage? It would be a smelly and messy job.

My great-grandfather had earned his living for a while dowsing for water. I knew little about him and this side of his work. Later he set up his own building company and became quite a wealthy man. Perhaps I had inherited his skills and interests?

I told Don I would be there. I also told him I had an idea about how to find the blockage. He accepted this without question.

Just as it was getting dark at the cottage and all the birds were in, I took my coat hanger rods into the paddock and dowsed. I roughly knew the track of the drains from the cottage to our own septic tank. By the time I had finished I knew exactly where the drains were. The rods responded in textbook style. It was almost a good game. I'd visualise a grid, then walk each square of the grid until I got a reaction. The rods would twitch and then swing. I placed a stone where this happened. I then walked the next grid, and did the same. Once it became clear that there was a straight line of reaction I narrowed my walking until I had a line of stones. I had no doubt that this marked the line of the drain from the house to the septic tank. Then I played about. It was like playing chase. I went yards away from the pebbles and started dowsing. I closed my eyes and meandered aimlessly. When I felt the rods move I opened my eyes… and there was a stone I'd placed. At one point it occurred to me that as I had taken most of the marker stones from the stream, they might be interfering with the integrity of the dowse. After all, they had been in water for years. But I was dowsing for, and had visualised, sewage drains, not water, so I discounted that.

Apart from digging up the paddock and some ground alongside the cottage there was no way I could prove that my line was in the correct place. Sally had forgotten where the drains had been laid all those years ago. So I had to take the results on trust. Nevertheless, once I had finished playing around I got pencil and paper, and drew the line as a record. I couldn't leave the stones there: they'd mess up the lawnmower and be kicked away by the poultry.

Job done! Tomorrow would be a greater test. The Crownes' septic tank was not as close to their house as Sally's was to hers, and there were also kitchen drains and run-offs with which to contend. However, I felt rather pleased that I seemed to have a result.

When Sally returned an hour or two later I was sitting watching television. I told her what I had done and she filed my piece of paper in with all her other pieces of paper to do with the cottage. We then tried an experiment.

I asked her to hide her keys somewhere in the cottage. I stood outside the back door with my eyes closed. When she was done I took my rods and asked them to guide me to the keys.

The rods reacted as soon as I went inside again. They pointed at a cupboard outside the kitchen. With a feeling of smug glee I opened the cupboard expecting to find Sally's keys. Not there. She was sat in the lounge watching TV, ignoring me. I was disappointed that I seemed to have got it wrong. I asked her if she had hidden her keys in the cupboard and it was just that I couldn't see them. No... the only keys in there were the ones to the cabinet where we locked up the shotgun. So: keys, yes. The right keys: no.

I had another go. This time I concentrated harder. I visualised Sally's key ring, car key, house keys etc. The rods began to twitch again. This time they seemed to take me into the back of the cottage, towards the Family Room. So that's where I went. As I got into the room the rods reacted more strongly. I stood in the middle of the room and slowly turned. The rods pointed directly at one of the sofas. There, underneath the seat cushion, were Sally's keys. Success.

So now I knew I could use my rods for a variety of purposes. I had traced drains, and I had found hidden objects. I knew that dowsing was not restricted to only looking for water. But my interaction with water was not done for the day.

The cottage does not have mains water. The supply is from either a spring or a well. It depends upon the whim of Padraig and Maureen his wife. Padraig has some sort of system in the Big Meadow whereby he selects from where the water will flow. There does not seem to be any particular reason for his choice. We suspect that Maureen likes to wind him up and tell him she cannot do his laundry this week until he changes the water. The cattle in the barn also affect the flow. Because the water is piped down the hill, and the pipes, which are shared by three house-holds, are not buried too deeply, if cattle wander over the pipes (which look similar to heavy-duty garden hose) then the supply is interrupted. The sign that this is happening is an erratic flow from the taps. Or no flow at all.

That night, as I was cleaning my teeth in the bathroom, the water came to an abrupt halt. As usual I tried turning on the other taps – kitchen and bath – to check they too were dry. They were. I tried turning all taps on and off suddenly, maybe attempting to uncover an airlock. Nothing. It was dark out so there was no point in traipsing up the field. We could phone the neighbours, but they might be in bed. So one more try and then hope it'd sort itself out by morning.

I went back into the bathroom and picked up my toothbrush once more. I turned on the cold tap and hit the copper piping below the basin. A dirty dribble spluttered out. Encouraged, I hit the pipe again. More flow, and a bit cleaner. So I leaned over and put my brush into the water.

As I leaned over the basin, suddenly there was a loud

gurgling noise. The water exploded out of the tap as if a dam had burst. But preceded by this torrent a large black... something – a leaf I presumed... slapped into the basin. I looked more closely. It was not a leaf. It resembled a slug. I called Sally.

"What's that?" I asked as she came sleepily into the bathroom. "Oh my God," she said. "It's a horseleech. But it's OK. It's dead."

There was no problem with the origin of our water. It was not a pipe blocked by cattle. It was a pipe into which a horseleech had climbed, or had been sucked. It had been swept through the plumbing and lain there, waiting; trapped in the domestic pipes, hoping someone would turn on the bathroom tap so it could make its escape. Lying there, letting water flow past it so that teeth could be cleaned, until...

I managed not to heave or feel too nauseous. And I did finish cleaning my teeth. With whiskey.

As I drove up to the farmhouse the next day I was both excited and anxious. The excitement was in anticipation of continuing to learn about dowsing; the anxiety was in anticipation of possible failure and humiliation. Of course I knew that the Crownes would not in any way intentionally make me feel humiliated; they both were open, non-judgmental, sensitive and genuine people: any feelings of failure would be mine and mine alone. Nevertheless, I did feel I was putting myself on the line rather. But everyone has to start somewhere, and where better to start than among friends? I had had a quick practice and that had sort of worked OK, what was the problem?

The problem was that I was 'winging it'. I was about to do something many people would consider oddball, eccentric, tricksy, supernatural etc, etc; whereas, in fact, it was something very natural and not at all oddball. It was just that it was new to me and I was new to it.

The day began in true Crowne style. We sat at the kitchen

table drinking tea and eating toast, surrounded by three cats and two dogs. Don cursed all politicians... British and Irish... who had no understanding of farms, farming and farmers. Ditto the European Union. A typical morning really. By now I could have written Don's script for him, I had heard the diatribe so often. Jane pottered about the kitchen, every now and then interjecting with a totally irrelevant point or asking me a question on another subject. But nothing stopped Don in mid-flow, and nothing prevented Jane saying whatever it was that was on her mind. For someone who did not know the Crownes the dynamics of their relationship and conversations were quite disconcerting. They appeared to either ignore one another or talk over the top of one another or dismiss one another's views. At times they would shout at one another, apparently oblivious to their surroundings and whoever was with them. But, as I had quickly discovered, this was part of their charm and there really was no deep-rooted animosity between them.

Meanwhile, outside the kitchen window, their ducks, hens and guinea fowl were scratching and squabbling, dust-bathing and resisting (or not) rape. Occasionally we could hear one of the horses from the field below the cowsheds. All the animals seemed to be relishing the early summer weather and getting the most from life.

When it was time to begin work Don raided one of the kitchen drawers for two supermarket plastic carrier bags. His wellington boots both had holes in the toes, so, especially for septic tank work, he needed inserts before he could put his feet into them. He also put on a pair of large rubber gloves that had been left in the porch. As his working trousers were well-darned and patched and held up with blue baler twine, he was doing a great impression of Worzel Gummidge.

Once correctly dressed, we crossed the yard to the raised part of the garden and the vegetable patch. This was where the lid to the inspection chamber was.

Lying on the earth near the chamber lid were several drain rods. Don had obviously been trying to clear the blockage. Even so, there was a foul-smelling and foul-looking seepage into the vegetable patch. This was not going to be a lot of fun. The only good news was that the day was dry, and not too sunny and hot. Rain or sunshine would have made the job almost unbearable. Don began to tell me his various theories about where the blockage, or blockages, could be. However, it seemed to me that all he could do was guess. Maybe the dowsing rods could provide a better picture of what was going on. So I suggested that he continue to do what he had been doing while I started to dowse the drains. He was happy enough with this suggestion so I went to my car and took out the old bits of coat hanger that had worked so well at the cottage.

After a few minutes of protection, concentration and meditation, I walked a grid pattern from the farmhouse, through the yard at the front, up the side by the old tennis court lawn to the vegetable patch. It took about three-quarters of an hour, checking, dropping stone markers, rechecking. It didn't help that the poultry seemed interested in what I was doing and moved several of my stone markers. Eventually I got pencil and paper from Jane and also drew out, roughly and nowhere near to scale, what I was tracking.

The rods were working well. I would get a reaction, mark it, check it, and move on.

I decided, for no apparent reason, to dowse behind the farmhouse too. Don had already pointed out for me where he believed the drainage and water pipes were buried; he had done some work on them years ago. But behind the house was not somewhere he had mentioned.

Between the back wall of the farmhouse and a large grassy bank there was about fifteen feet width of flattish land. It was largely scabby grass and strewn cinders from the fire in the lounge; Jane had a washing line there. The space was also used for storing various bits and pieces. For example, there were some old fence posts, a pile of builders' sand, old slate roof tiles, a piece of rusting farm machinery of indeterminate use, old breeze blocks, two traffic cones, a pile of scrap metal... Not an easy place to plot possible underground disturbances.

So now I felt compelled to dowse this place. I started at the house wall. If there were drains or water pipes then, logic suggested, they would enter the house. I walked slowly along the grass next to the back wall. At several points the rods twitched, but by the time I got to the other end of the house there had been no really strong reactions such as I had got earlier. Nevertheless I set off on a parallel path on the return journey, this time about three feet away from the wall. Again, twitches but not much else.

I decided that I would do two more runs, as any more than that would take me under the washing line and I didn't fancy dowsing while hunched up; less than that and I would feel I had not completed the task properly. I was losing my focus as it was.

On the final return trip the rods went berserk. Just at the point where the corner of the house extended towards the bank. This was odd because the twitches had all been consistent, and suggested old pipes near to the house; this extreme activity felt out of place.

I mapped out where the rods reacted the most strongly. In the end I had something strange: a pattern that was roughly rectangular and about four feet by twelve. Perhaps there had been an outhouse of some description? Or perhaps the soil had collapsed internally? I had no idea and by now had realised that such speculation was pointless.

I memorised where the anomalies had been and headed back to Don. He was nowhere to be seen. I heard movement in the old store shed, and I walked across the yard to find Don hunting through old feed sacks for something. "Ah, Simon. I thought I'd use the old pump. It's in here somewhere. How did you get on?"

I told him that I had finished but that there was one peculiarity. He didn't really seem to be listening, concentrating more on his searching. After a minute or so he stood up with what to me looked like a piece of mangled machinery with a bit of wire sticking out of it. "Ah, here it is. Time for more tea I think."

So once more we sat at the kitchen table while Jane brewed tea. The joys of being self-employed, I suppose.

When there was a lull in the conversation I again brought up the anomaly I thought I'd discovered at the back of the house. I explained exactly where it was, and the size and shape. I surmised that maybe there had been a sizeable collapse of soil and stones, and that underground pipework was damaged.

"Oh no," said Don, laughing. "I say, those rod things are jolly good aren't they?"

"It's not the rods, Don, it's Simon," put in Jane.

"Well... jolly good anyway. I know what you discovered down there. It's not pipes or anything. At least I hope not. It's Adolf."

"Adolf?" I queried. My mind raced with all sorts of speculation. "Who, or what, was Adolf?"

"Ah," said Don. "We must keep quiet about Adolf's fate."

More speculation, though I couldn't really imagine Don and Jane burying a body, be it German or a heifer, behind their house.

"He was a car," said Jane. "A Volkswagen. Beetle."

"And a good little runner he was too," added Don. "Except I tried pulling the horsebox with him and he sort of died on me. He was getting old anyway. And the cost of having him towed and destroyed was too much so I dug a hole and buried him. Out of the way. Round the back of the house."

I suppose the good news was that the rods had sort of worked for me; the fact that I hadn't sussed out what this lump under the ground actually was... well, I suppose I'd need practice. And cars did have pipes... Maybe I'd try a pendulum and asking 'yes' and 'no' questions. Something else to try at a later date. But for now it was back to the septic tank.

As we finished our tea I showed Don the plan that I had drawn. He was suitably impressed. He had not got a map of the pipes in and out of the farm, and me providing him with one would be helpful: especially if he were to want to bury more dead cars somewhere. However, it didn't really seem to indicate where a blockage might be. So, although it was a useful exercise in some ways, dowsing the farmyard had not helped move us forward with the septic tank. If I'd had more knowledge and experience with dowsing, I now know I could have found the blockage.

We spent the next few hours, either side of lunch, pushing hosepipe in and out of the foul semi-liquid that continued to ooze over the vegetable patch. When we weren't doing that we were digging up garden to find the tank itself. Every now and then there would be a glooping noise from the inspection chamber and a mini-explosion of air and bubbles would bring us hope, but eventually Don started up the small pump and began to pump from the tank down the drive. While it was pumping there was nothing we could do. So we went back indoors and had more tea.

While Jane was giving the poultry their afternoon feed, Don and I took it in turns to put rods down the chamber. Rod after rod was screwed together, twisted, pulled, twisted again, pushed and manoeuvred in every possible way. Various sucking and scraping noises continued to give us encouragement, but there was nothing obvious amiss. Eventually the pump had dumped enough for us to have a clear chamber. There were some fallen bricks resting in the half-pipe at the bottom, but nothing that should have caused a huge blockage. Don repaired the damage.

After a while Don went into the kitchen and turned on the taps, leaving me to watch for the water sluicing along through the chamber. There was no problem, but then there wouldn't have been. The blockage would have been between the chamber and the tank, but at least we felt we were making some sort of progress. Don came back to watch the running water.

"All we can do now is wait and watch," said Don. "Hopefully we'll have cleared something. I don't really want to take the top off the tank… that'll be a huge job."

Unfortunately, as we watched, the water started to back up.

Armed with two wheelbarrows and shovels, we proceeded to completely destroy the vegetable garden. With each shovelful of earth we knew how close we were to the tank because of the heaviness and liquid content of what we were putting in the barrows and wheeling off to the other side of the old tennis court. It was very hard work.

By late afternoon we had shifted enough for Don to be able to start lifting granite slabs from the top of the tank. Once more the hose and pump were put to use; this time with much greater efficiency.

It was time for Don to check up on and feed the livestock; it was also time for me to go home.

I went into the bathroom and cleaned myself up, conscious of the water running from the basin. Don had said he would finish the job on his own later. I had done all I could, so I felt OK with leaving him to it. We arranged that I would come over the following day and maybe help put everything back together. For now, that was it.

I said my farewells, collected my rods from their kitchen, got back into my car and drove to the cottage. Where Sally was already home.

I told her of my day, she told me of hers. We ate and went down to the hotel to have a drink and a game of snooker. I soon became aware of how sore my back was. Well, that was my excuse for losing. I wondered how I would feel the next day.

When I got to the farm in the morning there was great consternation. Don rushed up to my car before I'd even got out and told me that Lily had been missing all night. Had I seen her on the trip up the drive? I hadn't.

Lily was the collie sheepdog. A lovely temperament and a great worker. I remember a story Don once told me about her.

One hot summer day Don had taken Lily in his car to the Farmer's Co-op where he was buying bags of feed. She enjoyed the company and the change of scene. The Co-op is in Ballydrum, about eight miles from the farm. It is a group of large old buildings set beside the river.

When they got there Don went into the shop area, leaving Lily in the car with the windows open. He ordered the feed and was given his three-part chit to take into the stores. He drove into the store (a huge barn/warehouse with mountains of various grains piled up against the walls, and bags of feed on pallets). After the obligatory chat with the storeman he loaded the car boot with the bags of pellets and crushed oats and drove off.

It was only when he was halfway home that he realised Lily was not in the car.

He immediately turned the car around and drove back to Ballydrum. At the Co-op he pulled into the entrance way, over the weighbridge and parked on the concrete concourse. He jumped out of the car and began to call his beloved dog. No sign. He whistled. No sign. He went into the office and asked if anybody had seen Lily. Nobody had. He went into the store and asked the storeman if he had seen her. He had not.

By now Don was getting pretty upset. He half-walked, half-ran around the buildings, calling and whistling. Then one of the staff from the office came out.

"Sure, and isn't that the dog herself?" she said, pointing into the distance.

There, on the other side of the river, was Lily, running up and down the riverbank. Before Don could respond, Lily jumped in and swam back across. By the time she arrived on dry land again, Don was there waiting. He didn't mind the shaking wet animal; he just cuddled her as she jumped up and down in his arms, licking his face.

It was several weeks later that Don was able to piece together what had happened. Various sightings of Lily that day were reported to him.

After he had left the Co-op without her, Lily, who had jumped out of the car window, ran to the gates to follow the car. Indeed, if Don had happened to glance in his rear-view mirror, he would have seen her. Instead, as he drove off up the hill, she wandered back into the Co-op grounds. The car disappeared round the corner and Lily, taking the direct route, had swum the river and started into the village. She had been seen coming up the fields and into the Market Place. She was obviously making her own way home.

By this time Don had realised she was missing and turned the car around. Somehow Lily seemed to be aware of this, because she was seen in Ballydrum, when trotting along the High Street, to do a complete 180-degree turn and head back the way she had come. She knew where to go to be safely back with her owner.

But now I stood in the Crownes' yard, hearing that she had been missing for hours, presumably lost somewhere on the farm. She had never before failed to make it to the kitchen for bedtime.

Don had taken the tractor and driven around the whole acreage. Lily knew the tractor sound and, had she been nearby, would have come running. Or barked. But nothing. Jane had tramped the fields calling her name – stopping at places where she thought Lily might be hiding, playing or stuck. Nothing.

I could feel the distress turning into panic, and a sense of helplessness. Lily was much loved, as well as being a superb working dog. Don had done the basics that morning – fed the animals – but no other work would be done until Lily was found.

I had to walk away from Don and Jane; their agitation was too great. I explained that I would try to help, in my own way. Whatever that would be. So I wandered up to the farmhouse door, wandered around the front yard, wandered down to the first fields where the cattle grazed, all the while trying to distance myself from the high emotion, yet trying to tune in to what may have happened. And where Lily might be.

I stood gazing across the valley, taking in the trees, the livestock, the hillsides, the swards of shades of green and the ribbon of road in the middle distance. I tried to let a feeling of calm descend on to and into me. I carried out my protection routine. Slowly I felt a sort of bubble of peace surround me. It was like a giant soap bubble: multicoloured, reflecting prisms of light, gentle but hugely strong.

I walked back to my car and took out the rods. Don and Jane were nowhere to be seen. I took a few deep breaths and raised the rods, thinking of Lily. They started to twitch. Of course, Lily had imprinted her presence all around the farm. My problem was now learning to focus. To focus on the very recent past and the present.

I began to meditate, standing there beside my car in the farmyard. I very slowly rotated through a complete circle, holding the rods out in front of me. The twitching continued, but when I had been facing the house the rods jerked quite viciously. So I followed the rods.

They led me towards the farmhouse. How ironic, I thought, Lily was probably indoors all the while, asleep in the bottom of a wardrobe while frantic efforts continued outside to find her. But as I got to the house the rods moved from side to side, oscillating in front of me. They were actually pointing not *at* the house, but *through* it. They wanted me to trek up to the fields and walls behind; to the fields at the bottom of the mountain, where the sheep were let out on to common land.

So I followed. I trudged up the path beside the house, through the farm gate that separated domestic from working areas, past the copse of conifers that edged the neighbours' land, through the next gate and into the backfields: all the while the rods outstretched in front of me. And all the while they were leading me in the same direction.

Eventually I stood in the middle of the large pasture where often the Charolais bulls would be left. Fortunately the field today played host to only a few score sheep. I'm not really sure why I stood in the middle of the field; the rods were pointing to the side... beyond the stone walls, into the woods and scrubland of Don's other neighbour. The land where bramble and fir, gorse and bracken, stone and bog all merged into an untidy and apparently impenetrable mess.

If Lily was, indeed, in there, then I would have a real job finding her.

So, there I stood in the middle of an Irish field with old coat hangers in my hands, trying to find a lost sheepdog. Very different to teaching English to rowdy adolescents in Suffolk! But I knew which I preferred...

The rods were persistent and insistent. Each time I walked a pace or two, or turned to face another direction, they kept pulling me back to the same spot. But what was especially odd was that images of foxes kept breaking through into my mind. I had been keeping pictures of Lily in my head since leaving the cottage, so this was intrusive. Perhaps it was residue from what I thought I'd be doing at the Crownes' today... tracking foxes and protecting. Or perhaps Cernunnos was making his way into my consciousness, ready for the ritual of walking the boundaries. Or perhaps... who knows? I was learning to not question as often as I used to.

As I walked closer to the stone wall at the right of the field the pull of the rods became stronger and stronger; so much so that it almost felt as if they could be wrenched from my grasp at any time now. Although this was a new experience for me, I was completely convinced that the rods were pointing me towards Lily.

On impulse I thrust the rods down to my side and set back to the farmhouse. This time I did not stroll, I rushed. I felt compelled to hurry. Though exactly where I was going and exactly what I was going to do I had no idea.

Just as I got into the yard, by the stabling, Don and Jane appeared from inside the house. I asked them if Lily ever went into the backfield and over the walls into the scrub.

Jane went white. "Oh my God, Don," she gasped. "Padraig's traps."

The three of us ran up the track, into the field and to the wall. I pointed out where I thought the rods had been pointing.

"Don. Where did you put the traps?"

Poor Don was in a bit of a state. "I don't remember exactly," he said. "Padraig laid them and..."

"Not to worry." I'm not sure why I was so confident, but at least I could try to be reassuring. "Let's try the rods again."

Jane started calling Lily's name. She was running up and down alongside the wall. Don was looking both exasperated and very worried.

The rods pointed to a part of the waist-high wall where stones had dislodged from the top. Don saw this and started to clamber over the wall.

Jane was now alternating between calling the dog's name, shouting orders at Don and muttering incoherently.

I tried to follow Don over the wall but Jane ran over and grabbed my arm. "No, don't follow. If Lily is caught in a fox trap then Don's best on his own."

So, we stood and waited. Jane called out to Don every 30 seconds or so. Sometimes replies came, sometimes they didn't. Usually we could just hear Don shouting, "Liiillllllyyyy."

After a few minutes, or maybe longer, it went completely quiet. And I mean *completely* quiet. No noise of Don scrabbling through brush, bramble and bracken. No birdsong. No sheep or cattle cries. No wind in trees or distant cars climbing the mountain road half a mile away. Nothing.

I put my rods on the wall and sat next to them. Jane paced up and down, fretting.

We waited.

Then, like a train approaching from the distance, a roar. Jane and I both leaned over the wall, peering into impenetrable vegetation. We heard the sound of Don shouting but not the words themselves. We heard thumping, brushing and tearing noises. We seemed to see shapes and shadows; saplings quivered and branches rattled. And he appeared.

In his arms was Lily.

As Don struggled to get to us we could see that Lily was alive. He was pretty breathless as he tried to fight his way through by following the path that he'd made as he had entered the woods. Jane didn't know whether or not to try to meet him or wait. She called, "Is everything all right?" but by now we could see from Don's facial expression that there was a huge sense of triumph and relief. And that, indeed, yes, everything was all right.

When he got to the wall his grin was broad. He put Lily over the stones into the field, where she jumped up and down at Jane.

While Lily was licking Jane, Don shook my hand. "Thank you," he said. "Thank you. We'd never have found her for days but for you. She was in a live trap. One that Padraig set. Thank God it wasn't one of the snap-traps. God knows how she got there. She was just lying there. Waiting. Half-asleep. I think she must have been in shock."

After some minutes of shared mutual affection all round, we made our way back to the house. Lily was none the worse for her apparent ordeal and led the way, turning back every few yards to jump up at one of us. Without discussing it we all knew that we would be heading for the kitchen and a brew. Although first Lily would be fed and watered.

Once inside and our boots left in the porch, Don fossicked around in one of the tall kitchen dresser cupboards and emerged with a bottle of whiskey. He set three glasses on the table and poured. Jane, having sorted out Lily, who now lay dozing on her chair next to the range, was making coffee in a saucepan on the cooker.

I decided that I would not remind them that I was actually there to help put back all the soil from the septic tank episode. Instead I just raised my glass of whiskey and said, "Here's to Lily."

"Here's to Lily!" they responded, clinking glasses all round.

When she heard her name, Lily looked up, twitched an ear, and went back to sleep. Safe.

Chapter Four

Being woken at dawn is not something I enjoy, especially in the spring when the mornings are getting lighter. The cockerel crows were something I could tune out, but one early morning there was a big bang on the bedroom window that jolted me out of sleep. It was such a loud noise that I felt obliged to get out of bed and see what may have caused it.

Opening the curtains revealed nothing obvious. There was a mark on the window but I couldn't make out what it was. So I got back into bed and dozed until a reasonable hour.

Today was due to be quite exciting: Sally had ordered dozens of day-old chicks, and she was to collect them from the railway station. The stock of hens was getting old and while the foxes had been kept at bay, it seemed that the suicidal relationship some birds had with the lane outside the cottage was not something I could do anything about. Traffic used to be sparse but was greater now that the hotel was gaining in popularity. Perhaps if there had been a constant stream of cars then the hens would have been more wary; as it was, some insisted on pecking at the roadside verges and mistiming their return to base. Unfortunately the drivers of some vehicles also appeared to view the birds as targets. And most who hit a bird just drove on. So we would be indoors, hear a car, a light thud and upon rushing out on to the road see scattered feathers blowing and a hen lying motionless, and dead, on the road or on the verge.

There was no way we could completely prevent this without spending more money than we had on fencing and gates. I used to try talking to the birds, and every time I saw any wandering towards the road I would shoo them back; but chickens are not renowned for their intelligence or listening skills.

So now we would introduce some fresh blood into the flock and expand the number of birds. Having done some research we decided to buy some Bova Nera chicks. These are black birds which lay profusely. The nearest breeder was in Northern Ireland so, thanks to the Internet, we ordered and paid for six dozen. Our neighbours would have a total of four dozen and we would keep the rest.

I was looking forward to this experience. I had no idea how to raise chicks but Sally was well experienced so I knew all would be well.

I had bought bags of chick crumb when I had visited the Farmers' Co-op for the layers' pellets and goat feed the previous weekend. I had cleaned out the large wooden box which Sally had used previously as a nursery. I found the metal grille she wanted to use for a lid. Sally had been into the attic and returned with an infrared lamp that would be used to keep the birds warm. So I presumed we were ready.

Sally wanted to go to the station alone. She would pick up the chicks then drive around the neighbours delivering their quotas of birds. In the meantime I would investigate more thoroughly the noise in the night; and do the necessary with the existing stock.

As Sally drove off I made my way around the cottage to inspect the bedroom window from the outside.

There was definitely a mark, or two, on the outer glass. The double glazing reflection made it tricky to make out clearly what was there. It actually looked like claw marks, but that was ridiculous. None of the hens had been out and I'd never seen any of them fly that high. Perhaps it was somebody out early who had thrown mud or gravel at our window; though why anybody should do that I had no idea, but…

I went into the food shed and prepared the bowls of pellets and crushed barley for the poultry. I filled Circe's bucket with her feed and took it into the goat shed. She was lying chewing the cud and just looked at me lazily, if not scornfully. If she failed to finish her breakfast she would soon be raided by hens who seemed to prefer goat rations from a bucket in a nearby shed to hen food in troughs about thirty yards away. But that was Circe's problem; she knew what could happen. I suspect she actually enjoyed the company. Now that Sweetie was dead, the poultry were all she had for company most of the day. She was certainly amused by one of the cockerels.

Most of the hens were of limited character and adventureless. But we had a cockerel which was half-bantam, and I called him "Jagger".

When swapping eggs with neighbours, much is taken on trust. Obviously there can be no guarantees that what hatches will be female and a prolific egg-layer. But sometimes it happens that you end up with a bird that is not what you expected. Or wanted. And in that category comes half-bantams. They are nutters. (To use the technical jargon.) Especially the cockerels.

Bantams are small hens. They are often quite pretty birds. They can have fluffy leg feathers. Or be attractive colours. But half-bantam cockerels have a reputation for aggression.

At first we were not sure that Jagger was either bantam, or male. It is not simple to tell always straight after hatching. However, it soon became obvious that here was a bird that could strut his stuff. He would pose; he would demand female attention; he would attack other male birds; he would try to rape the ducks. And once he was grown and rather handsome, with his tail feathers glorious and his comb well defined and rich, he would have a go at Circe.

When Circe had her head in her feed bucket he would dance around her, hopping from foot to foot, head bobbing, crowing; and then he'd run at her, stopping a few inches away from her. There was no doubt Circe knew he was there. Usually she tried tactical ignoring. Sometimes Jagger would give up. Other times he'd just keep at it – until the goat would lift her head from the bucket and run at him. Then he'd show his true colours. He'd run away.

Unfortunately this would rile Jagger and injure his pride. So any human nearby would then be attacked. While this might sound amusing, believe me, a cockerel has sharp claws and beak. He can draw blood. As a defensive ploy, a well-aimed boot sometimes worked but keeping your distance was a more humane response. If it was not possible to keep distant because, say, work needed to be done in the paddock and Jagger was roaming with a beady eye out for either trouble or an unsuspecting hen, then avoiding eye contact helped. Though it's not always simple to determine what a cockerel is looking at. I did try reasoned argument with him. It didn't work. And threats only seemed to aggravate him. The worst tactic I tried was looking at him and saying, "Don't you dare." He saw this as a direct challenge to his machismo and got his retaliation in first.

When opening the hen shed doors to let out the birds in the morning, it was usually possible to tell what sort of mood Jagger was in. The hidden world of hen coop at night was always a mystery. Quite often sounds of shuffling, squawking and jockeying for prime perch position could be heard; but exactly what went on we obviously could not tell. However, when we opened the door any leftover group dynamics could spill out into the paddock. If Jagger was the first out it seemed to mean that he was now in charge. He would be eponymously 'cocky': which could mean he'd attack you for just standing there to prove his virility; or he'd treat you with disdain because he had far better things to do. On the other hand, if he was last out it meant he had not had things all his own way: we did have full-size cockerels that shared the shed… and he'd dash off in order to escape further embarrassment in front of his potential female conquests; or he'd attack you out of a sense of spite. So, there was basically roughly a one in four chance of being 'Jaggered' when opening the henhouse door every morning.

This morning was a morning when the odds were against me. I had poured the feed into the troughs and went to open the henhouse doors. One house had most of the female hens and the newer birds; the other had older birds and the three cockerels. The females' house was easy, but the mixed house could be a problem. I had got into the habit of unhooking the latch and standing behind the door as I pulled it open, thus putting the door at 90 degrees between me and the exiting birds. But this also trapped me between the door and the henhouse. Jagger came storming out. He saw me. He attacked me, flying at my shins. I caught him fair and square on the chest with a fairly gentle kick and he went staggering backwards and landed on his tail. While this was happening the other birds were coming out of the shed in various states of alacrity. Some hurtled out and went legging it up to the troughs; some sidled out and wandered off into the goat shed to have a go at Circe's bucket; some greeted the new morning with a gentle eagerness and walked across the paddock, stopping now and again for a quick preen.

By the time they were all out, Jagger decided that hunger was a stronger incentive than revenge, and he too headed up to the troughs. As he did so I went and let out the ducks. They had an advantage over the hens, which is why I let out the hens first: the ducks could fly halfway to the troughs, thus overtaking the slower hens. However, the problem with the ducks' enthusiasm was that as they left their house they'd kick the eggs that they'd laid that morning.

Hens lay in nest boxes: ours had private individual boxes (though they had been known to share) with access from their house; the ducks lay straight on to their bedding. Sometimes they'd build a communal nest… invariably right at the back of their house, thus making it really difficult to access and collect the eggs. Ducks also sometimes lay their eggs somewhere they thought was pleasant in the paddock; the hens had been known to lay in Circe's hay rack. It was always important each morning to count the number of eggs from both hens and ducks and correlate this to the number of birds. If the number of eggs consistently declined over a few days, this usually meant that the wretched birds were laying elsewhere. Not only did this mean fewer eggs for us to sell, it could also mean food for rats and crows: creatures we didn't want around.

So now I could collect the eggs. There was a reasonable number in each house and I was happy to take them indoors to wash. On a Saturday it was handy to have a total number of eggs for the week that was divisible by six. The butcher who bought our eggs preferred to have several dozen a week, but understood that we could not force the birds to lay according to his demand. Nevertheless there was no point in taking, say, 34 eggs to sell.

As I left the paddock I turned and looked to see that all was well. It was. The poultry were feeding happily... at least, the squabbles were only temporary... and Circe had her head stuck out of her shed. The weather was calm and fine and the first ducks to have finished their breakfast were in the stream washing: you could tell by the splashes seen above the bank.

I passed our bedroom window and had another look at the marks on the glass. I was still sure that they looked like claws. I was even more certain now – having just been mugged by Jagger it was possible to envisage a bird flying feet and beak first at the window. But I had never heard of this happening before.

While I was washing the eggs and sorting them into species (we got more cash for the duck eggs and not everybody appreciated them), I heard Sally's car backing into the driveway. I dried my hands and went out to meet her. She was just staggering in with a large, and noisy, cardboard box. As she passed me it became obvious that it was also a very smelly cardboard box. However, it seemed to be full of life.

She put the box on the lounge floor and joined me in the kitchen to where I had retreated in order to make tea.

Sally told me how she had been the centre of attention at the station – which she had enjoyed, explaining all about the chicks to waiting passengers; and she had also enjoyed a couple of hours of gossip at various neighbours. She had managed to turn in a small profit on the buying and selling of the stock. And now it was time for me to help move the chicks from box to temporary new home.

We put the large wooden box in the porch: the chicks would stay warm without getting too hot; they'd be safe from predators (except our cats, but they were not likely to get too excited about the new birds); we could keep an eye on them; the smell and noise would not be too intrusive as there was a door between them and the lounge; and, best of all, we could keep sneaking a look at them.

On the floor of the box we put fresh straw. On top of the straw we put three bowls: one filled with fresh water, the others with chick crumb. Then the grille as a lid. Over the grille, suspended by a piece of baler twine, we set up the lamp. It was guesswork as to how low over the box to put the lamp. To start with it appeared to be rather high, so we set the box on some breeze blocks, leaving the lamp dangling about 18 inches over the grille. If the chicks huddled together under the lamp they'd be too cold; if they dispersed to the corners of the box they'd be too hot. Using a cup hook or two as a makeshift pulley system, we were able to see to it that adjusting the lamp would be simple.

The chicks themselves were crowded into one large heap of black feathers in the centre of the cardboard box. By now they must have been thirsty, and possibly hungry. It had been several hours since they had been put on the train in the North. So Sally took them into the porch and began to transfer them into their new temporary home.

I had a go. I'd never seen, let alone picked up, such young chicks. When our own birds hatched we left them to it. But now we had to lift several dozen chicks, preferably without dropping them, from one box into the other. In fact it was easy. I was tentative with the first few but soon I became more confident and managed picking up two or three at a time and just swooping them into their new quarters.

Once ensconced they huddled together, squeaking and cheeping.

However, by the time the last chicks had been moved some of the more intelligent and bolder ones had discovered the bowls and were scrapping over feed and water.

We put the grille over the box, checked the lamp and left them to it.

I took Sally outside to show her the bedroom window markings, but she couldn't work it out either. I also told her of Jagger's continuing aggression. She laughed and said that he had never attacked her and perhaps it was "a male thing." I said nothing.

Later that day Gerald, Sally's elder son, phoned to say he'd be down from Dublin to visit for a few days with his new girlfriend. This always excited Sally so she was quite ebullient for a while.

By evening time we had kept an eye on the chicks several times. The lamp was now positioned in its right place; all the birds were alive; the feed required replenishing and the water topping up. All was well.

Outside, the scene continued as normal. Sally had cleaned out the bird sheds while I cleaned out the goat shed. Various broken boards had been fixed; various possible rat holes had been investigated and repaired. We had conducted a successful hunt for potential new perches – bits of timber lying around or bits of fallen branches from trees in the Big Meadow – for the chicks when they grew old enough to join the big birds outside. Over the next few weeks we could prepare one of the sheds for new birds; part of this process meant putting all the current hens into the one shed – something bound to stir things up.

As dusk approached, Sally put all the old stock away. Sure enough, a fuss ensued when some birds tried to get into their usual shed and found the door closed. They did not want to join the others in their shed; and the others didn't want them in either. Some of the displaced hens sought refuge in the goat shed. Circe was not happy about this. So she helped.

When we drove the hens from her shed they often avoided being driven into their house by dashing round the back. With two people this was usually just about manageable: one of us could act as a deterrent and shoo them back. Armed with long sticks in either hand, we stretched out arms to make us appear twice the size and the hens would turn tail in panic. But with hens in panic they lose any sense they may have had when calm.

So now life was a little more complicated. Lots of hens who felt displaced. Who resented not being able to get to their usual home; who were confused and lost; who did not want to share a house with the men hens. Consequently Sally and I could have been chasing them around for quite a while. We knew that once they were in, it would get easier each night; it was just the first time, now, that we had the most trouble.

But Circe came to the rescue. A wise goat. While Sally shooed from the front and edged hens out of the goat shed, I went around the back. If the birds came round the back they'd see me and leg it back to the front. Sally could then encourage them into the one shed. However, if they avoided Sally they'd reappear within my sight and do a three-point turn, usually with a dramatic skid, back. And so the cycle would go on. But with Circe standing her ground at the far end of the sheds, and shuffling from side to side, the birds were trapped.

It was a fun game. It didn't last too long as Circe was quite adamant that they "shall not pass". Eventually the three of us had won and all birds were clucking and crowing and crying in the same henhouse.

Circe was given lots of head rubbing and cuddles, and became very playful.

Playing with a goat can be exhausting. They are surprisingly strong and fast.

We ran round the paddock playing chase. Circe was expert at

the swerve and the sudden stop and take off. She could leap the stream and turn in a split second. If she allowed herself to be caught it was to play 'attack'. This is when I push her side and she pretends to put up with it. Then she turns to face me. She puts her head down and I either push her head with full force with my hand, or headbutt her forehead. The latter is more painful for me: goats have very hard and bony foreheads. Circe then rears on to her back legs and waves her front feet at me. This must be very scary for any foe. She stands tall, ears up, legs flailing. Not to be messed with.

Eventually we both give up the game, and huff and puff breathlessly. Even a goat gets out of breath and can cough like a dedicated smoker.

I hadn't realised that Sally had gone indoors. I said my farewells to Circe in the gloom and went into the cottage.

We had a quiet evening of television and chat, and went to bed at a reasonable hour. However, yet again we were woken in the early hours by banging on the window. This time I leapt out of bed and drew aside the curtain. I was just in time to see a crow flying off and perch on the fence on the far side of the paddock. I returned to bed. I had just dozed off again when, again, there was the bang on the window. This was starting to make me cross. No longer bemused, no longer intrigued, I lay in bed plotting how to prevent this happening any more.

Of course, it really depended upon why this wretched bird seemed so determined to be a 'window-crasher' into the cottage. But it was probably futile to speculate. And somehow it seemed inappropriate to call upon Herne. So defensive action had to be taken.

While Sally tended to the chicks after breakfast, at her request I set about taping newspaper and black bin liners to the inside of the windows. Sally's theory was that the crow could see its reflection and thought it was attacking a rival. I wasn't too sure about this; but then I wasn't sure about anything to do with these events so I dutifully, rather than with enthusiastic commitment, taped the bedroom windows and the patio doors. I then went outside to work out if I could see my reflection in the glass. I could. So I taped more bin liners to the outside of the windows; thus darkening the inside of the cottage, but hopefully deterring further crow attacks.

The Bova chicks had all survived the night and seemed settled into their new temporary home. Sally and I watched as they jostled and scrabbled among themselves, rushing to the food or water and then dashing back to the shelter and comforts of the corners of the box. All these chicks should have been female: they were birds that could be sexed at birth according to their colouring. But even now there were one or two which looked suspiciously to have brighter heads, and combs, than their peers. But it was early days yet. And the breeder had put in a few extra: presumably in case of fatalities or incorrect gender identification.

The day passed quite calmly, for us. In the paddock Jagger was still on the occasional rampage. No birds were zapped on the lane outside. And I went to the local garden nursery to buy some plants.

We had decided that the fencing between the front lawn and the lane was too easy for the birds to get through. Also, there were large gaps under the sheep fence on the bank that was intended to keep Circe in. A solution was blackthorn.

When we had been expecting goat kids, Sally had found a supplier of free fence poles. A local builder of garden sheds ordered rough six to eight foot long pine poles from the sawmills. Sometimes splitting them down the middle to create rustic walls damaged them. Sally was given trailer loads of poles which I had then used to block up possible kid-sized escape routes from the paddock. However, there were only enough long ones left over to form fencing around the weeping copper beech tree and the willow tree that I had planted. These needed to be fenced to prevent the saplings being eaten by stray cattle or an escaped

Circe. The remaining bits of pole we kept: they'd be useful for something one day.

So now I was planting thorn all over the place. I had about a hundred plants. And a good strong pair of gardening gloves.

I started out the front, digging small holes with my trowel and just dropping in the nine-inch high baby bushes. It was not too strenuous and rather tedious. However, after an hour I had established a production-line type routine and was quite skilful.

I then went into the paddock to plant the rest. The ducks were nowhere in sight: presumably up the Big Meadow somewhere; the hens were sitting around, dust-bathing or pecking in the paddock grass, and Circe was lying in the sun.

I lay all the remaining blackthorn plants on a piece of sacking beside the lowest part of the bank behind the birdhouses. There were already some thorn bushes under the sheep fencing, but they were sparse in number and poor in quality of growth. So fleshing them out with more would be appropriate. I began digging into the stony soil with the trowel.

The routine I had established swung into action. Dig hole. Reach behind. Grab twiggy bush from on the sacking. Plant said bush. Fill hole. Dig next hole. Reach behind etc.

After a couple had been planted I would drag the sack along to the next six feet or so of bank, and swing into action once more.

However, on the third move I turned to move the sacking to find... nothing.

About six feet away from me, and with a glint in her eyes, stood Circe. Beneath her lay the sacking. Between us were scattered dozens of baby thorn plants. And Circe was chewing.

Without me hearing or seeing a thing, the goat had sneaked up and helped herself to some juicy snacks. And now she was challenging me, hopefully in fun, to recover them.

I didn't know whether to chuckle or shout. So I played her game and pretended mild outrage. Circe ducked her head as if to charge. I lunged towards her and she backed off. I ran at her. She dodged back and stood over the sacking.

We played at this for a few minutes but eventually I got fed up. I grabbed the sacking and started to bundle the remaining plants into it. Circe stood a distance away. If I left the plants in order to get a rope with which to tether her, she'd start eating or moving them again. I first had to ensure their safety. Then I'd get her!

Which is what I did. I wrapped what was left: which, to be fair, was a goodly number, in the sacking and put them on the highest part of the roof of the bird sheds. Hopefully out of reach of a determinedly playful goat. I went into the feed shed and found the tether. But, of course, Circe saw this coming and legged it to the other side of the paddock. But that was OK. All I had to do now was ensure I was vigilant.

By dusk I had planted all the thorns. Of course, Circe would probably pull out the ones she could reach, but at least there was now more infill. And with the windows and patio doors taped, it felt a little like we were preparing for a siege.

The Bova chicks... which I now called "the Bovver birds"... were growing almost before our eyes. They were certainly thriving. That evening Sally and I cleaned out their box, putting fresh straw down before replenishing the food and water dishes. The night-time temperatures were still low, so we had to keep them in the house with the warmth of the lamp. In a week or three it might be possible to put their box in the feed shed, complete with lamp on extension lead. Although the cover of their box would have to be rat and cat proof. But for now they remained in the porch.

We slept right through that night. No dark visitors attacking the windows. Perhaps Sally's ploy had worked in spite of my reservations about its efficacy.

The following morning Gerald, Sally's son, phoned to say he couldn't get a lift down from Dublin after all. So Sally offered to drive up after work on Friday (she was on evenings so would finish at midnight) and bring him here on the Saturday morning. She'd then drive him back to Dublin on Sunday afternoon. Terry, his younger brother, was going away for the weekend with his girlfriend. Gerald's girlfriend was working this weekend.

The next few nights we were attacked again. Bombed by a bird. The darkening of the windows had only worked temporarily. So what now?

I really only had one tactic left.

Using the remnants of the half-poles of shed timber that Sally had acquired, I built a wooden barricade, or stockade, along the paddock-facing wall of the cottage. It covered the windows and the patio doors. And looked rather ridiculous. But I had fun.

The first night after doing this all was silent.

The following night, the Thursday, there were thuds in the night. On Friday morning my inspection of the poles showed holes in some of them. The crow had flown full force: claw marks, beak marks and small holes of indeterminate origin were to be seen in the wood. In some ways it was amusing, in others scary, and also frustrating. I didn't want the bird, or birds, to be harmed... but neither did I want us to be bombarded in the early hours.

However, having watched the weather forecast on TV, I had high hopes that tonight I'd be free of any Hitchcockian drama. We were forecast to have a storm with very high winds. Hopefully all crows would remain at home.

Storms meant checking everything was secure. Before Sally left for work she helped me dismantle the window stockade: it was ineffective and may have been dangerous in high winds. We also tidied around the paddock, weighting down anything that could possibly get blown around. It was an opportune time to ensure the heavy-duty polypropylene (the material builders use under concrete floors to ensure watertight barriers) that formed the outer skin of the roofing on bird and goat houses was properly fixed. So I got the staple gun out and spent an hour on the stepladder, firing into the various shed roofs.

Jagger was not impressed and stalked menacingly around the bottom of the ladder while I was working on his house. I was tempted to use the staple gun as a disincentive for him; but that was only a fleeting shadow thought. He seemed to realise I was working in his best interests, and he left me to it when I climbed back down to earth.

As well as trying to minimise potential wind damage, storms could mean floods for us.

The wash-off from the hill behind us could lift the water level in the stream from a pleasant, pastoral tinkle to a raging torrent within an hour. When in spate we could hear the rocks we'd used for dams to make duck ponds trundling along the stream bed. Sometimes we could watch lumps of paddock eroded and washed away into the road. There had even been occasions when the sheds were flooded: putting hens at risk of drowning. However, usually we managed to keep the stream within its banks. Judicious placing of stones and rocks combined with good maintenance and water management techniques ensured the drama of heavy rainstorms did not turn into crisis.

So when Sally had driven off to work I spent the rest of my time outside ensuring the run-off stream – "Stream Two" I imaginatively called it – was clear. I went up the hillside to check my configuration of dams would be effective and that the trench I had dug to take overspill was clear. It took water down to the road across the grassy bank by the back door. This lessened the load the main stream had to carry.

That evening, having put the birds away and fed Circe, I settled down to a quiet night in front of the TV. I lit the fire and chilled out with the cats. Just before I got ready for bed I checked on the chicks. All was well. Already the wind was picking up and the rain starting. I was looking forward to snuggling down into the warmth and having a peaceful night.

But it didn't happen like that.

It was about 2.30 in the morning that I awoke. The light from the clock radio was flashing and as I registered the fact, it went out completely. A power cut. Not unusual for the middle of the Wicklow countryside, especially when the weather was bad. Snow, ice, heavy rain, gales... all could lead to a power cut of several hours. And tonight I was alone in the cottage: apart from dozens of young chicks who needed warmth to survive. By now I was fully conscious. It was cold, dark and noisy... from the wind outside. Cold. Chicks. Oh dear.

I had a flashlight beside the bed and I eventually grasped it. I pulled on a dressing gown, considering options as I did so. Although I knew we had a camping gas stove, I wasn't happy about lighting that and leaving it in the porch. Apart from anything else, the thought of Sally returning to find scores of chicks dead from fumes was not a good one. The central heating was no good: although I could try to relight the lounge fire, the electric pump wouldn't be working. So I guessed that a slightly more primitive solution was called for.

I went into the porch to find the chicks all huddled together in a corner of their box. It was cold in there. I picked up the box and carried it into the lounge, setting it in the middle of the floor. I closed the door to the porch to keep the cold air out, and the door to the lounge from the kitchen corridor to keep the cats out. I then went into the other bedroom and took the duvets from the bunk beds. I wrapped these around the sides of the box, using cushions and pillows to keep the duvets in place. I didn't want to suffocate the chicks by covering the lid. All this by torchlight; and it was very dark and rather wildly noisy outside.

Once I was satisfied I had done the best I could, and I was starting to shiver, I went back to bed, praying that they'd all be well.

A few hours later and I was awake again. Still no power, but natural light was seeping through the bedroom curtains and I realised it was early morning. The clock was still off but my watch showed it to be 5.15.

I got up and went to check the chicks. They were spread out in the box and there was the occasional cheeping noise; they seemed well enough. I considered re-setting and lighting the fire but it seemed too much hassle for so early in the day. So I looked out of the windows to see what the storm had done... and was still doing.

It was a mess. And highly dramatic.

There were fallen branches of all sizes spread everywhere before me. I went around the inside of the cottage, looking out of every window. The wind was still blowing strongly and I watched as branches as thick as elephant trunks hurtled vertically across the paddock at head height. Fortunately even the ever-curious Circe was nowhere to be seen. The lane outside the cottage was blocked by tree limbs twenty or thirty feet long. The fence between the stream and the Big Meadow was spread-eagled beneath a melee of various tangled wood. The duck shed had been missed by what looked like inches. Actually in the Big Meadow I could see gaps where I knew that the previous night there had once been trees. Where Sally usually parked her car there was now half a tree; my car had only a few twigs on its roof, caught in the aerial. We had been so lucky. Or blessed.

It seemed that the wind was gusty rather than a continuous blast, and it was coming from the direction of the lane at the front. Therefore it seemed safe to open the back door. Which I did.

My lungs gasped as the strength of the passing air hit me. It brought back memories of when I was in sixth form at school and used to ride pillion on friends' motorbikes... no crash helmet and 70 mph on the road between school and the rugby pitches where we'd play for the pride of the school on a Saturday morning. The bruising passion, volatility and mix of excitement and fear: it all came back to me as I stood in the back porch. I quickly went back inside.

After breakfast – a sandwich and orange juice – I pondered my next move. It was the weekend and later there may well be traffic down to the hotel. The ducks and chickens would need letting out: but not until there was less chance of them being blown across the fields like litter on a deserted city street. Circe would be OK for a while, too. Sally wouldn't be appearing for hours – if she could even get back. There was no telling what the roads were like further upcounty. I wondered how Don and Jane were doing on the farm, but the phone was as dead as the power. The Bovver chicks were fine. So there was not a lot I could do. And I guessed that Padraig would be out with the tractor soon to clear the road.

Wrong. After a few hours of reading, the time now was near to nine o'clock. No sign of anyone anywhere. The wind was easing; it had eased to a normal gale and it looked as if anything that was going to fall down had probably fallen by now. So it seemed safe to go out and see the damage close up.

Where to begin? Well, at least we'd be OK for fuel for the winter... plenty of kindling and logs.

I began to collect the smaller branches and twigs and put them in a pile on the grassy bank. Then I got fed up with the twigs and concentrated on the larger branches. Soon I had quite a pile and I had not even cleared from the back door to the front lawn.

I wandered on to the lane. Debris was scattered in both directions. There was so much fallen timber that I didn't know what to do with it. The larger pieces I hauled either back to the cottage for later sawing up or on to the verges. The largest pieces I could not move. So I went back for the bowsaw and made them manageable.

Eventually I had cleared a hundred yards or so, and, provided they were careful, cars could negotiate their way along the lane. Not that there were any cars. But even some of the sturdier standing trees had bits of other tree stuck in their branches. I was nervous about how much of a hazard they were. However, I could do nothing about them, so was just wary as I walked up and down the lane, sometimes tugging, sometimes carrying, as I did my neighbourly bit – and claimed the salvage of winter fuel.

I was relieved that I had taken down all the protection from the windows. Bin bags and poles had been neatly stacked away safely – not blown around. With a bit of luck the recalcitrant crow, or whatever it was, had been blown away by now.

Once I had cleared as much as I could of the lane and its immediate environs, I tackled the paddock. I had been right in my observations of the duck shed. The birds had escaped crushing by inches. One of the ash trees had uprooted and crashed on to the paddock fence, its limbs resting on the duck-shed roof, its trunk across the stream and smashing the fence. I would have to move it some time: it was blocking the stream and any rain soon would mean flooding; also there was just enough space for either Circe to escape into the Big Meadow, or, admittedly less likely, Padraig's livestock to wander into the paddock. But for now it would have to lie there. I was too tired and muscle-worn to move it, saw it, chop it or do anything else to it.

It was getting on for lunchtime. I let out and fed the ducks and chickens and gave Circe her bucket. She showed no inclination to come out of her shed, so that was fine.

I went back inside. Still no power. Still no phones. It would all happen when it happened: which could be anything between a few hours and several days. Mobile phone signals were unobtainable from the cottage; to make a call required either a climb up the hill behind for twenty minutes, or a drive up the lane for five minutes, to where the ground was higher.

I decided that after I'd eaten it would be interesting to drive up the lane to see the scale of the damage elsewhere... as well as to see if I could contact Sally. Or the Crownes.

Another sandwich. More orange juice. Then with mobile phone into the car.

No vehicle had passed the cottage all day, so I was expecting to see plenty of debris, if not complete blockages. However, it wasn't as bad as I expected. Yes, there were signs of trees down. But I had not been the only one out doing some clearing up. I parked in a small lay-by on the edge of the forestry, where they grew the Christmas trees. Presumably the saplings had been young and supple enough to withstand the excesses of the storm, because there was relatively little damage. I switched off the engine and dialled Sally's mobile. Her phone was switched off. I left a message. I then rang the Crownes. They only had a landline so – surprise, surprise – I got a message from Eircom saying the phone was out of order. I phoned the emergency number for ESB and listened while their recorded message told me that they had no idea when the power would be back on.

There was no more to be done back at the cottage so I decided to venture off to the farm to see if the Crownes needed, or would like, some help. This also appealed to my sense of drama and adventure.

The roads were not too bad. It appeared that some neighbours had been out with tractors and cleared. However, the track up to the farmhouse was a different matter. There were large branches blown all over the fields and lying across the potholed driveway. Several times I stopped the car, got out and pulled large bits of tree out of my path. Within sight of the house, however, there was a whole tree right in front of me. I had three choices: try to move it – but there was no chance of that; drive around it, and risk getting bogged down in the muddy field – a possibility, but I didn't know for sure whether Don was at home so if I got stuck I'd have to stay there until he arrived with his tractor; and finally… the option I chose… walk.

It wasn't very far now, only a few hundred yards. I was wary, though, in case any weakened branches decided to use me for target practice as I walked along. I also hoped that my car was not going to be in the way if Don had indeed got busy with the heavy gear and was somewhere behind me, rather than ahead.

Much of the fencing along the track had been torn down. And one of the field gates was scattered in bits. There was no stock to be seen in any of these unsecured fields, so I presumed Don had moved it.

I rounded the final bend and could see the house. In front were the two tractors, parked beside the raised flower beds outside the front door. Also parked, round the side of the house, was Don's car. So they were in, even though the front door was, unusually, closed.

As I passed the final two fields I realised that they had more sheep in them than normal. So that answered one question. The cattle would, I had no doubt, be in the cowsheds.

Closer to the house now I could see that the reason for the Crowne phone being out of order was that the line had been bestraddled by half a tree. The phone pole was at an angle and the line was hanging limply and broken, while many branches lay on the ground between two poles. However, generally there was not too much indication of storm damage around the farm or the house.

I guessed that both Jane and Don had been up in the early hours, sorting out stock, checking for damage, tidying around – whatever needed to be done. None of her ducks or hens were out, and it was late morning already. But I bet the livestock had been fed… otherwise I would have heard ovine and bovine complaints as I now opened the farmyard/garden gate. There was no sign of Lily either. Nor Grouchie, their whippet. It was customary for all visitors to be greeted by the dogs. But not today.

Just as I got to the front door it opened.

"Well hello there," said a cheery but bleary-eyed Don. "How're you doing?"

"Fine," I said. "And yourselves?"

"It was quite a night, wasn't it? Come on in and we'll get the kettle on. The power's just back on."

An hour later all three of us had had several mugs of tea... made on the solid fuel stove, with toast and jam. Jane went out to release her birds while Don took me on a tour of the worst of the damage.

There was no major demolition; no great rebuilding required. Nevertheless, there were many hundred yards of electric fencing to repair. One break anywhere along the run and the whole lot was useless. This was an opportunity to re-fence most of the fields... if I was prepared to help. I was.

We arranged that I would come up to the farm the following morning and spend the next few days digging holes for posts, running wire between them, mending broken wire and repairing gates. But for now we would move the tree from the lane and get my car turned around and headed back to the cottage. Then I would phone Eircom from my mobile (which required leaning out of a bedroom window to get a signal) to report the phone line down. And phone Sally to ensure she was back home safely.

It didn't take long for us to clear the track. Don used ropes and the tractor. He left a trailer alongside the track and, as he drove back towards the farmhouse, I used the chainsaw to start to make the detritus into something useful: fence posts and firewood.

After an hour or so I put the saw in my car and drove up to the farm. I put the saw in the shed, said my farewells to Don and Jane, declining an offer of more tea, and headed back to the cottage.

As I topped the hill above the cottage I caught a glimpse of Sally's car. She had obviously got home safely. I pulled up, backed into the far drive and parked next to the caravan. The birds were happily doing their thing in the paddock and Circe was rubbing her side along the paddock fence. A scene of pastoral normality. The only sign of the turmoil from last night was the tree over the fence the other side of the paddock, leaves and twigs still scattered almost everywhere and the gap in the trees in the Big Meadow.

I went indoors to find Sally and Gerald ensconced in front of repeats of *The Bill* on television. I greeted them both cheerily, got absorbed grunts in return and went into the kitchen and boiled the kettle.

That night I went to bed relatively early. Certainly Sally and Gerald stayed up a lot longer than I. Sally was well practised at creeping into bed when I was asleep; her work shifts meant this happened regularly. Still, it was past two in the morning when I heard the TV switched off, followed a little later by the latch on the bedroom door lifting.

About three hours later there was the now familiar sound of the local double glazing-hating big black bird: a schizoid psychopathic suicidal attack beginning again. Perhaps it had Japanese ancestors with some sort of karma associated with kamikaze?

I could only doze for the next hour or so and got up earlier than I wanted, or I felt was healthy for me. I checked on the chicks, showered, had breakfast and watched breakfast TV for a while. Then it was into the car and the short drive to the Crownes. I didn't bother to check the bedroom windows for signs of the attempted invasion.

I had an interesting time there, tiring but stimulating – more of which in the next chapter – and arrived back at the cottage early evening.

Again Sally and Gerald were watching TV. I had a shower and changed out of my working clothes. It was getting near dusk. I asked if the birds had had their afternoon feed. They hadn't. So I went out to do the business. Circe was hanging around outside the feed shed as I approached the paddock: usually a sign of her hunger.

I opened the paddock gate and was immediately besieged by dozens of apparently starved fowl. I shooed them to one side as I went into the shed and loaded corn into a container.

After they were fed I went to Circe's shed to collect her empty bucket. By now the goat herself was three-quarters of the way up the paddock, trying to open the gate to the enclosure where the bird feed troughs lay. There had been a time when she used to be successful: the latch being weak and simple. But now I had improved the security and wrapped twine several times around the gate and fence post. A nuisance when opening and closing the gate, but definitely Circe-proof.

I put Circe's evening feed in her bucket and left the feed shed. As I did so my eye was caught by a black shape blowing on the earth where the hens used to dust-bathe, right next to their shed. I walked up to it, realising as I got closer that it was a bird. The wings were fluttering, otherwise it was motionless. And dead. And headless.

I felt my heart beating. Fluttering almost in time with the dead bird's wings.

I took the bucket into the goat shed and left it there. I returned to the corpse. Sure enough. It was a large hooded crow: probably, presumably, the very bird that had been attacking the cottage. But now dead, and without its head. I admit to feeling a little sick... not out of squeamishness, no, more a mixture of feelings: not least anger and also real sadness. It was so unnecessary. I could guess what had happened. If I had picked up the body and examined it I was certain I would discover lead shot peppering it. And where the neck was exposed on the body there was a clean cut. The head had been cut off. Deliberately.

I left the paddock and walked the path alongside the cottage, wondering whether or not to say anything or what to do. I got to the back door and decided I was still too upset to see Sally and Gerald. As I paused in the back porch, rehearsing possible scenarios, I heard the sound of their laughter. That decided me. It was so irritating that I stomped away, climbed the fence to the Big Meadow and went for a walk.

It was daft... after all, it was only a crow, and a bird that had caused us hassle and nuisance. I should have been glad that we'd now be left in peace. So why was I upset? Why wasn't I pleased? Over the next twenty minutes or so I calmed down. The fields, the trees, the grass, the stream, the bracken, the greens and browns, the clear air, the distant views, the sounds of birds and sheep and cattle... all smoothed away the churning I had felt. Eventually I found a fallen log and sat on it, staring at the hillsides across the valley, watching the silhouettes of swooping birds, the apparently miniature houses and toy livestock. I had had a good day at the Crownes... only to be spoiled when I got back home. Or, rather, I was letting it be spoiled. Yet, somehow, maybe what I had experienced on the farm that day helped me now. Before I moved on I apologised to Pan, to the crow faerie, to the angel of birds, to Herne... to whoever/whatever... for what had been done. I felt a bit foolish but then I felt a bit more peaceful.

I sauntered back down to the cottage. There was no sign of human life; the hens were starting to gather at their sheds, waiting for permission it sometimes seemed, ready to go to bed. Circe was munching grass. The ducks were not yet in the paddock... but looked as if the single file military-type line was preparing to march down the Meadow, under the fence, across the stream and up to their shed.

I took a deep breath and headed indoors.

Gerald was still watching television but Sally was in the kitchen cooking dinner. She was watching and stirring something on the stove, and turned round to greet me as I walked in.

"Hi," she said. "Won't be long now."

"Fine," I said and sat down at the kitchen table. "Everything OK?"

"Thanks for feeding the birds. No need to put them to bed. Gerald'll do that."

"OK."

"He shot the crow this morning. Good, eh?"

"I saw the body."

"He's got the head so he can keep the skull. He has a collection of skulls. He'll put it in bleach and then display it."

"Right."

"So we shouldn't be bothered at night any more."

"Right. Good."

"How are the Crownes?"

"Fine. The usual. I enjoyed the day there."

"Dinner will be ready in about 10 minutes."

"Good. I'm hungry. Been a busy day."

"Eat in here or in front of the telly?"

"Here's good."

"Gerald?" she called. "Birds. Dinner."

Sally took plates from the cupboard while I set the table for three. I heard Gerald switch off the television and head for the porch. For some reason I felt compelled to leave the kitchen and go into the Family Room, from where I could watch him through the patio door or windows as he put the birds away for the night. I didn't tell Sally and I kept out of Gerald's sight.

I arrived at the window just as Gerald was opening the paddock gate. All the poultry were ready and waiting. Gerald walked across the paddock, presumably to do the ducks first. As he did so two things happened.

Jagger erupted from the midst of his harem and flew at the back of Gerald's legs. Gerald had obviously not heard Jagger coming and stumbled forward, startled. Jagger then retreated a few yards while Gerald recovered. Bearing in mind what had happened to the hooded crow earlier, Jagger's behaviour did not seem to me the brightest. Fortunately Gerald seemed to decide against immediate retaliatory action, though as he continued towards the ducks he kept turning around to check he was no longer being mugged by a half-bantam cockerel.

By the time he got to the duck shed, I was aware of the second happening. Because my attention had been drawn to the drama of man versus chicken, I hadn't noticed – not seen, nor even more strangely, heard – that all along the fence between the Meadow and the paddock there sat crows. Perched on the sheep wire and on the fence posts were dozens, scores maybe, of black birds. All silent. All watching.

Gerald had put away the ducks, closed the shed door and turned to move towards the hens. They were behaving quite normally now, just hanging around outside their shed.

Then there was a moment. A tiny moment. A split second, maybe a whole second, or two… I don't know exactly. But everything in the world outside the Family Room window seemed to stop. To pause. To draw breath. To be a snapshot in time and space.

The hens stood still. The crows stood still. Gerald stood still. The air in the light of dusk seemed to grow, to expand, to get heavy and uncomfortably warm. It was silent.

And then normality returned. Like a cinema full of people who had held their breath as the hero suddenly overcame the death-defying predicament he was in. Or maybe it had been the film projector that had held on to one frame of the movie for just a fraction too long and now was released. Whatever. Gerald saw the crows and did a double take. As he did so, with one accord they took off from the fence, each one making its evening cawing noise, and flew over the paddock and back up to the top of the Big Meadow where they always roosted.

At that point Sally called, "It's ready." I watched the birds for another few seconds; I saw Gerald shooing the hens into their shed: they went obediently; I turned and went to eat.

During dinner Gerald initiated nothing in the way of conversation. Sally burbled away quite happily; Gerald and I made the right noises in response. As we were finishing he told us that Jagger had attacked him; he asked if the bird had had a go at anyone else.

"See," said Sally to me in mock triumph, "I told you it was a male thing."

We explained the recent Jagger history. Gerald then suggested that he get rid of Jagger. He offered to wring his neck.

I waited to see what Sally's reaction would be.

"I don't really think that's necessary," she said, somewhat tentatively.

"But he's a crazy. He's nuts. Psychopathic. He'll do damage," protested Gerald – more serious than joking.

"We've lived with it OK," I said.

Now Sally was in a quandary. "Maybe we do have too many male birds?"

"You're the expert," I admitted, "but…" I was about to say something along the lines of maybe there'd been enough bird-killing for now; was it really necessary; wasn't Gerald overreacting etc. But I held back.

"And he is a half-bantam. His progeny might be as bad as him." I wondered just who Sally was trying to persuade.

"OK then. Leave it with me," I said. "When you get back from dropping off Gerald it'll've been sorted. I'll do what has to be done."

Gerald looked a little disappointed.

So I asked him, "Everything alright when you put the birds in just now?"

"Er yes. Fine. No problem. Apart from Jagger. Bastard." And he laughed a nervous chuckle.

The Bova chicks would soon be ready for their first real trip into the outside world. There were many of them and only one Jagger… so my priority was to ensure the safety of the little ones. I had a plan. I would get rid of Jagger… but not in the way that Gerald may have been considering. All I needed was an evening alone. And I would be getting that tomorrow: when Sally was in Dublin.

That evening we went, at my suggestion, to the hotel for a

game of snooker. We had a mini-tournament and when I was knocked out, leaving Sally and Gerald to play, I went for a walk. I had a good scout around, gathering the information I wanted. When I returned to the snooker room the game was nearly over.

Next day I was the first one up. I had breakfast and went outside to do the birds and goat. It was a quiet sort of day. No rain, but no bright sun nor wind either. It was like yesterday had never happened.

After feeding the livestock and gathering eggs, which I left in a bowl on the windowsill of the feed shed, I returned to the crow body. I got a spade that had been leaning against the shed wall and picked up the bundle of black feathers. I carefully walked over to the old 50-gallon oil drum we used as an incinerator and left the spade and dead bird on the concrete next to it. I collected the egg bowl and went back indoors. Still I was the only person up and about.

I went quietly into the kitchen and put the eggs on the drainer, ready to wash them. We dump burnable trash next to the kitchen bin in old feedbags, which I now picked up and took outside, having first put a box of matches in my pocket.

I emptied one bag of trash into the incinerator, plumping up papers and cartons so there was adequate air to keep them burning. Then I gingerly picked up the spade and leaned the blade over the edge of the oil drum. The crow slid off and landed amidst the rubbish, half-disappearing as its weight took it down. I piled in the next bag of flammables and arranged them so there were bits of paper sticking out, ready for me to light.

It took three matches and nearly-burnt fingers to set the lot alight. Soon flames and smoke swarmed almost vertically from the oil drum, with dollops of flying ash scattering across the paddock. Within a few minutes it had died down to a gentle oozing of grey smoke and I could peer into the depths to ascertain that the cremation had been successful.

I spent the next hour or so tidying, sweeping, cleaning. I

replenished the water buckets for birds and goat. I checked that the thorn I had planted had not been 'Circe'd'. I searched the entire paddock for any eggs that may have been, literally, mislaid. Finally I got into the stream and fiddled about with rocks and pebbles, ensuring the integrity of the pond dams for the ducks.

I decided that I would need one more reconnoitre before this evening. As I went indoors to change from my wellies into trainers – safer for driving the car – Sally came out of the bathroom. We greeted one another and I told her I was popping down to the hotel briefly. She told me that she was about to take Gerald back to Dublin. They'd go to the cinema and then she'd take him back to his flat, where she'd stay till tomorrow. I hadn't expected that they'd go so early in the day, but wasn't completely surprised. She said they'd not be at the cottage when I got back.

So, having just said hello, it was now time to say goodbye.

I parked in the hotel main car park and walked around the grounds. I concentrated on the stables and orchard – which is where the hotel let their own hens run – trying to look casual and innocent. Which, of course, I was. I suppose that really none of this was necessary; if truth be told I was enjoying the subversiveness of the whole thing. The scheming and plotting, the planning and anticipation. Perhaps I didn't have enough to fill my life!

When I got back, the cottage was empty. All livestock was now my responsibility. I checked the Bova chicks and discovered empty feed and water bowls in the box, so filled them. I put the kettle on and looked in the fridge to see what was left for my own feed. Not much, was the answer. As usual, Sally had taken much of our stock up to Dublin. When I looked on the windowsill I also found the fruit bowl empty. And when I looked on top of the kitchen cupboards all the crisps had gone too. Fortunately the supermarket would still be open so I made a quick list and headed into town for a shopping trip.

This didn't take much more than an hour. When I returned home I unpacked and made myself something to eat. I indulged myself and sat for a while in front of the TV for an afternoon of (almost) uninterrupted sport coverage. The only interruptions were when I fed the cats, washed all the dishes and went out into the paddock to give the poultry their second feed of the day. I also lit the stove so that during the evening I would have the friendly warmth and glow of the fire. I anticipated sitting there, pouring myself a small whiskey, or two, once I had accomplished my mission.

When dusk approached I put on my boots and went out to do the birds. It was a straightforward exercise and all went well; all hens went in the one shed and the ducks were well mannered and obedient. I fed Circe and found another empty grain bag in the shed. I put the bag on top of the henhouse and went back indoors. It would take a few more minutes yet before I could start.

The birds usually settled down quickly. If they were put to bed too soon they would squabble. If you stayed out in the paddock pottering it was possible to hear the occasional squawk and complaint; when these stopped it was safe to assume the birds were roosting happily. A gentle stroll past the henhouse should then elicit no more than a fluttering of feathers or a chirrup. By the time it was truly dark there would be no noise at all.

I went back inside, pulled the curtains and made myself a cup of coffee. I was beginning to feel a bit nervous. Our relationship with hotel staff, and owners, was good. We were invariably made to feel welcome. When we treated ourselves at such times as a birthday to a meal in their extremely good restaurant, it was not unknown to be given a free bottle of wine. I didn't want to undermine this.

I lifted a curtain and peered out. It was now dark enough. I found the torch and stood in the back porch putting on my wellies. With a single beam of light guiding me – fortunately the weather was cloudy and there was not much moon – I locked up, put the keys in my pocket and trudged alongside the cottage, past the old caravan still full of junk and went as quietly as I could into the paddock.

I shone the light on the henhouse to check that the bag was still where I had left it. The light must have disturbed the birds: there was a shuffling noise and the odd chirrup and cheep.

I carefully lifted the bag from the roof and put the torch on the stones in front of the shed, its light shining skywards. I heard movement beside me and looked around. I was just able to see Circe with her head sticking out of the shed, peering nosily. I could do without goat interference right now.

I had seen Sally do what I was about to attempt, but I had never tried it myself. She had had years of practice. I was hoping for first time lucky.

As I opened the henhouse door I realised I was holding my breath. One advantage that Sally had when doing this was that she was shorter than I. Bending down I looked into the gloom, trying to spot which birds were on which perches. Jagger was at the front. Yes!

The birds started to get slightly agitated. I wasn't sure what would happen if I really upset them. I was in the doorway with dozens of hens in front of me. I was blocking their way to escape. There was no time for thinking such things. Now I had to decide whether to be wary and careful or to just go for it. I chose the latter. Like at the dentist: just get on with it and get it over with as soon as possible.

I grabbed Jagger's legs and turned him upside down. I quickly turned, banging my head on the inside of the door, and plunged him into the feedbag. He struggled briefly and then lay still. The other birds squawked and nudged each other, but soon all was calm again. I closed and bolted their door.

I held the bag by its neck and lay it on the stones, putting my foot on the opening to keep it closed. Rather than knot the bag itself, I tied some baler twine round the neck.

Triumphant, I picked up the torch. Light in one hand and a bagged Jagger in the other, I left the paddock and opened my car. I had left my trainers ('runners' is the Irish word) in the back of the car. I quickly changed my footwear and settled into the driver's seat. I looked at the bag on the passenger seat. There was no movement and no noise. I just hoped that the psychotic cockerel that I was rescuing was still alive. It would be ironic if I had killed him by mistake.

Resisting the urge to poke at him, after all it was only a few minutes' drive, I set off to the hotel.

I had already sussed out where to park and where to release the bird. There was a short path amid flower beds and shrubs, leading from the main drive into the hotel to the back of the stables. Although it was dark and the hotel's birds would be inside and roosting, I expected that Jagger would be safe enough for one night. He would probably settle in the middle of one of the shrubs. The chances of him being foxed were slight as there was usually plenty of light, movement and noise to disturb any possible predator. Anyway, I felt that all would be well: Herne was on my side now. I hoped. Well, he ought to be. I was saving a mad hen from certain death; he could take his chances for just one night, surely…

I parked the car on the road and just sat there, waiting. Some of the stable workers lived on the premises, and I didn't want them to look out of the window just as I was doing the deed.

After a few minutes I took the bag out of the car, closing the door as quietly as I could. I walked up the road and turned on to the path I had noted. There was just enough light from one of the street lamps that lined the driveway for me to see where I was going. When I was halfway along the path I stopped and looked around. It is not that easy to appear nonchalant whilst carrying a white feedbag containing a cockerel. I'm not sure I managed it.

Anyway, I rested the bag on the path and untied the twine. I aimed the mouth of the bag at a nearby large bush. I shook the bag gently and a somewhat bemused Jagger tumbled out. He didn't even stop to look around, preen or try to restore some personal dignity; instead he made a dash for the middle of the shrub and disappeared from my view.

I stood there for a few seconds, wondering what to do. Then I bundled the bag into as small a ball as I could, tucked it inside my jacket and walked back the way I had come.

When I got back to the cottage I felt tense and nervous. The adrenalin had kicked in by now. All sorts of doubts and questions raced through my head. So I poured myself a whiskey and sat by the fire in the near-darkness.

I felt a little calmer after a while and spent the next half hour on the computer in the spare bedroom. I surfed the Internet and played a few games of FreeCell. I then had a go at Gran Turismo on my PlayStation and won a couple of races on the rally circuits.

Before going to bed I checked on the Bova chicks. All was well. I hoped that now Jagger was gone we would be able to put the chicks into the empty shed very soon.

And so it proved. When Sally returned from Dublin I told her I had "got rid of" Jagger and that I was not going to tell her any more about that. In this way she would not be compromised if the truth was discovered. Within the week she had decided that the Bovvers could go into their own shed, where they would remain locked in while they became acclimatised to their new home. It was a simple task to carry the box into the paddock and slip the chicks straight on to perches in their new home. We put food and water in there and shut the door. There they would remain for a couple of days.

It was strangely calm in the paddock without Jagger. The pecking order adjusted itself, and life continued as if he had never existed. Soon it would be time to introduce the new birds to the old. And let the Bovas discover the routines to which they would become accustomed.

One weekend, when Sally had been working the day shift the previous week, we felt the time was right. We could both be up at a reasonable hour and oversee the assimilation of the two populations.

The troughs were filled and ready, but this time with enough for three shedloads, rather than two. For a change I let the ducks out first. Sally then opened the door for the older hens at exactly the same time as I opened the door for the Bovas. Sally's shed emptied as usual. The Bovas just sat, or stood there, blinking in the morning light. Presumably they were anticipating that I would be taking out their bowls and refilling them. They were now in the habit of eating and drinking in the same place where they slept.

I stepped into their shed and began shooing them out. They didn't like this and kept hurrying back in. We were going around in circles. So I left them to it. I hoped that hunger would get the better of them and they would emerge in their own time in order to forage.

Which is exactly what happened. Watching them do this also gave us the chance to see which birds were leaders or the most brave, and which were wimps. Sally and I stood just outside the paddock, leaning on the gate and commentating on the scene. It would be interesting to see how the new birds settled in with the old – although at the moment it appeared that ne'er the two should meet. And I couldn't help but wonder what it would have been like had Jagger still been there.

As the day progressed the Bovas became bolder and ventured further from their house. It was possible to watch them from the Family Room window, rather than stay out all the time. An occasional few moments at the window assured us that the new birds were all OK, but had still not found the feed troughs. They were scrabbling around the paddock for food and sometimes they wandered back into their house looking for food. But their bowls inside the shed were empty. They had water bowls scattered around the paddock, but the food was more of a problem for them.

By the time for afternoon feeding, all the Bovas had come out of the shed. The more daring ones had ventured about fifteen yards from their house, but still not found the troughs. Of course it didn't help that to get to the troughs they had to cross the bridge over the stream and duck under the fence of the enclosure where the troughs now were. But they did have the other birds to lead them, or show them. However, it was as if each set of birds totally ignored the other; as if the others didn't exist. So I had to come up with a plan to ensure the new birds got fed properly every day.

I told Sally my plan and she agreed to give it a go. I went outside and caught Circe. I tethered her to a tree along the road verge. There she could browse but, more importantly for now, be out of the way.

We left the afternoon feed until about 90 minutes later than the previous day's. When Sally and I both appeared in the paddock, all the older birds rushed to the gate and the feed shed, jockeying for position, pushing and shoving, shouting and complaining. Several nearly got walked on. The Bovas stood quite still, apparently totally perplexed by the furore.

Sally put feed in a bucket and started up the slope of the paddock to the stream. The older birds followed. I walked up to the nearest few Bovas and picked them up. Bending over and treating them rather like a human toddler playing with a doll, I walked them, in pairs, up the paddock and across the bridge. With their claws just touching the ground and their heads bobbing from side to side, I did this with the majority of the birds. It was a back-breaking exercise for me... but they didn't seem to mind. Once on the other side they were able to find their way to the troughs. We had been able to leave the gate open because Circe was no threat.

As the Bovas approached the troughs, the other birds made

way for them. They were accepted immediately. All the Bovas stuck together and all the older birds stuck together. When all the feed was gone and some of the older birds began to leave, younger ones followed. Soon there was a posse of hens, young and old, black and brown and white and mixes of all three, crossing the planked bridge back down to the paddock.

The Bovas were at a disadvantage when it came to the water buckets. Because they were still young and small they couldn't reach over the lip of a bucket to sip. So on the way down to the henhouses it was the old gang who stopped to drink. The newer birds had to wait till they were almost back home... to where the saucers and pans of water were laid.

For a first foray into the world of grown-ups, or at least of adult hens, the Bovvers had all done well. Of course, the real test would be in the morning: would they remember where the feed was.

No they didn't.

The next morning I let out the Bovas first. They stood around, bewildered. Then I let out the ducks. They did the usual panic half-running and half-flying thing. When I opened the third shed door all the incumbents shot out, scurried past the rather foolish-looking newcomers and legged it up to the troughs.

Once again I transported the small black birds in pairs, carrying them a few inches above the ground, moving their legs for them as we crossed the bridge – if any of our neighbours had seen, then 'laughing stock' would have been more than apt.

However, this time there were a few more intelligent Bovas who began to follow me as I headed across the bridge and up to the troughs. But they weren't that intelligent... because they also followed me straight back, without getting to the feed.

Eventually they were all trained. That evening it required minimal intervention on my part, and after two days nobody would ever have known the lengths I had gone through on behalf of a few dozen chickens.

I dread to think what it would have been like had Jagger still been on the loose.

We discovered a few weeks later that Jagger was alive and well and had not changed in the least. In fact, what I discovered gave me a twinge of guilt... but in an unexpected way.

When the weather was warm and the evenings lighter, and when Sally's shift work permitted, we would go down to the hotel and get a bar meal at the pub part of the hotel complex. We could sit out in the orchard and eat *al fresco* under a picnic umbrella. Amidst their chickens. Their normally child-friendly, hospitable, well-adjusted chickens. But this time was different.

We went into the bar and ordered as usual, then went to sit outside. There was always a series of round cast-iron tables under large sun umbrellas. Families, couples, friends could all be seen, smiling, eating, drinking. Giving crumbs and leftovers to the chickens that ran among the chair legs and pecked at human feet, or to the hotel dog that was as good a beggar as you'll ever see. But when I looked at the table where we decided to sit I noticed a piece of paper taped to the top. It appeared to be on every table. It read, "Warning. Most of our hens are friendly but please remember they are not pets. Do not allow children to run at them. One hen, we call him Elvis, will attack if provoked." Well. There you go. Jagger had settled in, been renamed but not rebranded: he was just the same old half-bantam, aggressive, unpleasant, untrustworthy...

I showed Sally the note. She smiled and said, "Aha." I asked her to ask no questions or say anything: she was supposed to be ignorant of what had happened. But I told her I'd ask the staff who brought us out our meals what this was all about.

A few minutes later that is just what I did.

We were told that the bird had just arrived one day; they had no idea from where. He was soon running with all the other birds and was 'a bit of a problem' at times. Because he would attack people. Including the staff. And customers' children. He'd also had a go at the hotel dog... a large, elderly, dopey Golden Labrador. They'd called him "Elvis" because of the way he walked. I asked what his likely future was; the answer was a small smile and a shrug of the shoulders.

The weather was warm and sunny for the next couple of weeks. The Bovas settled in brilliantly. Eventually some even mixed with the previous population of birds and all seemed calm and cheery in the poultry world around us.

Sally's shift pattern meant that we didn't get to eat at the hotel pub for another three weeks. We had almost forgotten about Jagger/Elvis, so when we sat outside in the orchard waiting for our meals to be set before us, I was surprised when Sally asked if any of the other tables had the 'Beware of the Chicken' note. Our table didn't.

I stood up and casually walked around the tables, smiling benignly at the occupants, returning to Sally with mixed feelings. There were no notes. So either Jagger/Elvis was now well behaved, or more likely...

I felt guilt that I had imposed him upon customers and their children: there might be families scattered throughout the world (the hotel was internationally known) who were now hen-phobic. Yet he had had a few more weeks of life. I had given him another chance. It was hardly my responsibility that he chose to continue to be antisocial. But perhaps it had been my responsibility to ensure his life was ended humanely. I had – dare I say it – chickened out.

It was a different waiter who served us this time. I tried to be relaxed as I enquired over the whereabouts of the "cockerel that had been a bit vicious. Elvis I think he was called." He was a little hesitant in his response. But he knew us; he had seen us there on several occasions, so he must have thought it was safe. Setting our plates down, the waiter picked up a menu from the table. He scanned the list. He put the folded card in front of me and pointed. I had to get out my reading glasses. His finger was indicating "chicken curry". We exchanged knowing smiles and he left us to eat our dinner.

Chapter Five

I have mentioned the rather magical day I spent at the Crowne farm, and now, perhaps, I had better write about it.

It was after the storm. I had agreed to help them repair some of the damage, mainly to the fencing. So I set off early and dressed in my farm labouring outfit.

As usual, as soon as I arrived we sat at the kitchen table and drank tea and ate toast. Jane was keen to talk about a calf that had been born two nights ago and was not feeding. It didn't seem to know how to suckle and its mother wasn't able to help. She was highly anxious, and both she and Don seemed to expect the calf to die. They had tried manhandling the calf on to the udder, but the baby just couldn't hold on and suck. Neither would it take a bottle.

I felt that they were hoping that I would volunteer to help… but I wondered if this was arrogance on my part. They were the farmers with years of experience; I was just an unemployed teacher and counsellor. But they were friends, there was an animal's life at risk: so I offered to do what I could. I did have a little animal healing experience… albeit with a goat that I knew. So, tackling a calf I didn't was a step up I suppose. Just that bit more of a challenge.

Jane showed me the stall where the mother and calf were. I opened the gate and just stood there. I had been warned that the mother might get very stroppy: she may not be feeding her baby, but she could still be very protective. And cattle are heavy. And strong. And can kick.

I leaned against the block wall and watched. The calf, a bull, seemed to be sleeping. I closed my eyes and asked for help. It is like reaching upward into the unknown, into the universe, and hoping, or expecting, that someone or something will respond in the way requested. Or maybe it is just a way of consciously becoming much more relaxed. Whatever it is, it works. And it worked this time.

When I felt the time was right – whatever that means, but then I knew the time was right, somehow – I knelt down next to the calf. Mum turned her head and looked down at me. Apart from that she remained motionless. I put my hands over the calf and tried to visualise him sucking. He stirred a bit but didn't move. Then I started to think: or at least, thoughts were put in my head. I don't know which.

Are animals subject to karma? My first response was that they are not. Karma is about cause and effect. It surely requires conscious actions; and just how conscious of their actions are animals? They mainly work instinctively. We have different rules and a separate morality for animals. And can animals be moral? Or immoral?

I guess that animals have a collective karma: a sort of tribal destiny. They are not as individuated as we are; yet there is no denying, as anybody who has kept pets will know, they can show signs of individuality. And this is true for farm animals, too: so with pets it is not the influence of close proximity to humans. Perhaps extinction of certain species is an example of animal karma?

So why was this particular calf likely to die? Well, that's just the way it is. We are significantly different to animals; which gives us that extra responsibility. Towards other people as well as towards all living creatures. And my responsibility now was to do the best I could for this particular calf in this particular place at this particular time. Why should this calf suffer? Aha... the 'why suffering?' question. Again. And anyway, what do we mean by suffering? I have had pet cats with cancer; they have seemed to be uncomfortable rather than in pain. If human, we might call their attitude 'stoic'; but is that an appropriate term for an animal?

None of this was doing the business for the calf. I let my

hands do what they wanted over the calf. And I tried to stop my brain from intruding. This was a problem I was becoming used to: were my thoughts my own – in which case were they ego-derived, intellectualising or intuition? Or were they thoughts 'put there' by... whoever, whatever. Trying to differentiate was never easy. It was like what happens when meditating. Things 'drop in'. But their point of origin and their subsequent significance was usually a mystery to me. Another example of trying to learn to accept and not question.

The bull calf stirred more. He struggled to get to his feet. So I helped him. And I placed him under his mother, his mouth next to her udders. He just stood there. I stroked his throat and under his chin... as if he were a cat. He seemed to like this – but still stood there. This could become pretty annoying... but being annoyed didn't seem appropriate to healing, so I tried to push my patience button.

He stood there. Mother stood there. I knelt there, stroking. The calf leaned into an udder so I put it in his mouth. Still nothing happened. So I kept on stroking while calf stood there stupefied and mother stood there apparently oblivious.

After a minute or so she turned her head and licked her offspring. I had no idea whether or not this was a good sign, but at least something had happened!

And then calf pulled away, bent its front legs and lay on the straw again.

While my wish to help may have been, in part at least, fuelled by compassion, I was also getting pretty fed up – if you'll excuse the pun. Exasperation is not necessarily a positive thing to feel when with animals: they do not see nor experience the world in the ways we do. Nevertheless, I had to draw upon my years of teaching experience to take a deep breath, bury my frustration at this apparently stupid or stubborn or bloody-minded creature and try again.

Which we did. Many times.

Calf lifted up, udder in mouth, calf stands still, mother getting more bewildered, calf lies down...

I tried for over an hour. I asked for help from the cow angel (!) or whoever, whatever, could help. I visualised until I could hardly tell what was really happening and what was in my imagination. I drifted off into my own world. I came back to this one. To find that nothing had changed.

I was beaten.

We all were. Don. Jane. The mother cow. Me. And above all, the calf...

I was sore and stiff from lifting and holding the wretched beast. I determined to try one last time, so I spoke crossly and aloud to the little bugger that this was his last chance to get it right. After this he would be on his own, and up to now he had shown no signs of being able to do what was necessary so I didn't expect much. I told him he would be letting down his mother, the Crownes, me, the whole bovine population...

He turned his head on the straw, blinked at me and tried to stand. I helped him up. Mother licked him – and me – as I put his head to the udder. He shuffled forward. He opened his mouth... yes... this was going to be it. I could feel it. Triumph. Then he slumped to the floor.

I stood up and left the stall.

Knowing when to quit is a lesson I was conscious of learning. It's true when counselling: especially when counselling adolescents. Sometimes enough is enough. For now anyway!

So I wearily and stiffly made my way back indoors where Jane was tidying the kitchen. She was unsurprised, but naturally disappointed at my news on the calf; she just asked me to tell Don. Apparently he was out in the fields somewhere, so I went to look for him.

I followed the sound of the tractor up to the back of the house and into the field where the bulls were sometimes kept. It was several acres in size, bounded by stone wall on two sides, one of which was the boundary to the mountainside where Don had grazing rights for his sheep: gorse and fencing on one side and just fencing, with a gate, on the access side.

As I went through the now open gate I watched Don take the tractor up the right-hand side of the field, parallel to the wall, dropping off large poles en route up the hillside. This was obviously to be where he wanted the new fencing.

I wandered over to the wall and stood next to the huge roll of sheep fencing and tools that apparently he'd dropped off first. I could see that logs, or poles, had been dropped off at regular intervals. Some of these poles still had bark on them, so I assumed he was recycling the fallen trees which he had chain-sawed last night. I foresaw a day of really hard work ahead.

And I was correct.

I told him of my failure with the calf. He seemed phlegmatic and pragmatic about it, though I knew he was sad; and sad more for his beasts than for the money he would lose. But, as he said, "Life goes on... let's get on with it..."

The first thing I was instructed to do was debark the bottom few feet of each pole. I had a hand axe and a sort of large slashing knife to choose from for this job. When each pole was clean I then had to dig a hole, drop in the pole and backfill the hole. Then Don would help me stretch the sheep wire between the poles, and the fence would be nearly done. The finishing touch was to cut small bits of timber to nail at 45 degrees to the top of the poles, cut a notch and run single-strand wire along; this would subsequently be electrified. Each pole was roughly seven feet tall, the girth greater than my upper thigh and had to be very well secured in the ground: bulls would rub against the poles and were more than capable of bringing down a loose fence. They had already done some damage to the stone wall: hence fencing in front of it as well as round the rest of the field.

I got to work with the axe, stripping bark from the sections of the timber that were going to be buried. I managed to finish one post while Don, using the slashing knife, did two. But that was OK... it was his farm and his field.

While Don walked off up to the next post, about ten yards away, I began to dig a hole for the first post in the corner of the field.

He had given me a spade and a wrecking bar: something like a large, long crowbar. It was this that we had used previously when lifting large stones and rocks from out of the garden near the septic tank. I presumed it was to remove rocks from the neighbourhood of the hole I was digging. I also had a pair of strong gloves.

I selected the general area. It was right in the corner: one side was the wall, that continued downhill into the next field; the other side was grass banking, gorse and numerous shrubby things set among various trees, none of which I could identify. There were old fence posts and dilapidated wiring running along the top of the bank. The wall also had vegetation growing in, around and on top of it; perhaps that contributed to the fallen stones that littered the base.

We would lose a few feet of field, but I looked for a specific place that would minimise this, yet also provide a secure foundation. I dug my heel into the ground to check its softness. All seemed fine. I picked up the spade and pushed it into the grass.

I soon had a pile of earth and stones excavated from a growing-in-size hole. Occasionally I needed the bar to caress, persuade, then gently lift a large rock from out of the hole; but the scrabbling with gloves and a bit of effort – and a few grunts – while kneeling down was always rewarded with a sizeable chunk of stone being dumped on the pile.

To check the depth was adequate, I decided that putting the pole in and then extracting it again was foolhardy, so measured my progress on the bar: setting that mark alongside the bottom of the post. It is surprising how deep a hole may appear to be –

until you want to bury something in it.

About twenty minutes after I first started digging, I felt the hole was ready.

I walked away from it to scan its position. There would be no going back once I had decided that this was where the corner post was going. I looked at the place from alongside the wall; I looked at it from alongside the grassy bank; I looked at it from many yards away in the open field. Fine.

Don was nowhere to be seen so I took it upon myself to lift and lever the new fence post into position.

While it was leaning in the open hole I did the survey again. Yup... all was well.

I began to pick out stones from my discard pile and pack them around the base of the post. I thrust them down with the spade, adding earth, until I could get the heel of my boot into the upper part of the hole and tamp them hard. The post was no longer leaning; the hole was no longer a hole.

Once I had completed the first post, I pushed it and tried to rock it back and forth to test its rigidity. There was a tiny bit of movement but basically, I thought, I could feel some pride. So I stood back and admired the work.

As I did so I thought I heard a noise in the shrubs to my right – along the top of the bank. It sounded as if it was somewhat larger than a bird rustling through the leaves, but I could see nothing. Perhaps it was a rabbit. Or weasel. Or... whatever. All I cared about was that the re-fencing had started and I had made a good job of the first one. However, there were dozens more to do.

Somewhat stiffly – I was already aching again – I made my way up the field to where Don had dropped the next pole. I carried the spade and dragged the bar behind me.

Soon it would be lunchtime, but for now there was time, probably, to get the next post fixed. I dropped the bar and lifted the spade, ready to cut into the grass. But, again, there was a rustling sound – this time from the gorse around the top of the wall. I slowly rested the spade on the grass and stood still.

I waited.

Quietly.

More noises. Shadows also, this time. Movements amongst the vegetation. Then stillness and silence.

I waited some more. But nothing else to hear or see. Or imagine. Yet the hairs on the back of my neck were standing on end. It wasn't fear. It was more like anticipation... but of what I hadn't a clue.

I plunged the spade into the soil and it hit resistance, sending vibrations into my wrist and up my arm. It hurt. I swore and dropped the spade.

I heard laughing. No doubt about it. Laughter. I looked around, rubbing my arm. Nobody there. I swore again. More laughter. It was high-pitched, but I couldn't tell if it was male or female, old or young. This time I seemed able to determine its location: the other side of the wall. Some halfwit had been watching and now took delight in my pain. Whoever it was must be pretty determined: the gorse on the wall was thick and prickly, and the scrub and shrub on the other side were pretty substantial. I knew there was at least one path through it as Don's neighbour – Paddy C – used it as a short cut when coming from his farm to visit.

I sidled up to the wall and peered through the bushes. I could see nothing except foliage and wood.

Checking my watch I saw it would soon be time to head back to the farmhouse for lunch. I shrugged, leaned the spade and bar alongside the wall, and put the axe on the topmost stones. There was no sign of Don, no tractor to be seen or heard, so I started to trudge my way across the field. As I did so, I heard barking and Lily came bounding through the distant gate and headed towards me. We greeted one another and walked back to the house, Lily half-jumping and running backwards as she played with me, no doubt the dog believing she had successfully rounded up her target.

While sitting and chatting to Jane as she completed making lunch, there was the sound of a vehicle arriving in the driveway, a door slam, a knock on the door and in walked Paddy C. Whoever I had heard laughing up in the field, it obviously hadn't been Paddy.

Close behind him, Don hurried in, pulling off his wellies as he stood in the porch. He and Paddy were not only neighbours, they were good friends and helped one another out. Don helped Paddy with his animals and Paddy helped Don with heavy machinery. It was an arrangement that suited them both: each using his strengths to support the other. Don was often popping over to Paddy's to help, especially at lambing time, even though he had many ewes to deal with himself; and Paddy would appear with some sort of JCB or big mechanical digger when there was need at the Crownes. Unfortunately, once they were together they would talk farm-speak... which effectively excluded me, and sometimes Jane too, from any conversation.

What interested me this time was that Paddy was telling Don about mink that he had seen. Mink are a pest. They kill newborn lambs, apparently for the fun of it. When a family of mink move in to an area they scavenge for a few weeks and then move on. I hadn't realised that not only did they like to be around water-courses, they could actually climb trees. They are also quite terri-torial, but males travel much further than females: many miles. Males will have several dens scattered along a route. However, a family of mink in any area is bad news for anyone with small or young livestock. Especially if it is either mating or birthing season. Now that Paddy had definitely seen one... which is not common as they are shy and avoid people... the news would go around the valley and the guns would be ready and/or traps set.

"And you'll need to watch out for sure," he directed at me. "What with all those chickens and ducks by the stream. Your mink will be up there like a shot."

A number of thoughts and pictures flashed through my head all at once: Cernunnos, Sally, walking the boundaries for the protection, shotguns...

"Sure and don't you know Michael, up at Glencummin?"

I said I did; it was Michael who had helped us out with Circe on the mountainside.

"Ah, well, I think you'll find he is your man for a trap. If you want one that is. This mink won't go that far up the valley. He's had them there before now."

I stored up this information and after lunch I went back to my digging holes and filling them with fence posts.

All was quiet for an hour or so. Methodically I worked my way along. Eventually I came to another corner, furthermost from the rest of the farm. This was truly the boundary.

I had paced myself reasonably well, but by now my muscles were aching. I slowed down a bit. I sat on a grassy bank and looked out across the valley, over the trees, the land... some farmed, some not. I could just about make out the caravan in the front garden of the cottage where I now lived. The clouds were high and moving faster in the sky than the amount of breeze on the ground seemed to suggest.

It was so peaceful.

I got to thinking about how it was I got here. The journey of the last couple of years. Perhaps this is the time and place to recount that tale.

Sally and I had known one another for more than 30 years. We had been in the same Youth Drama group where we grew up: in Bristol. We had gone out together for most of our adolescent years. It was a special relationship for us both; one we each cherished.

Over the years we had gone our different ways, but managed to meet up every couple of years or so, always in England, as well as talking on the phone occasionally.

One day a couple of years ago when she phoned me – I was

living in East Anglia at the time and a senior teacher – she was obviously really upset.

It transpired that the man she was living with, Dermot, was becoming more abusive and the worse for wear for the drink. Sally had lived with him for many years – after her divorce from her children's father. I, too, had been divorced.

By this time I was qualified as a counsellor and had worked with difficult children for a while. I found I was using my professional training and experience on the phone to help her out. It was clear that the end was in sight for her relationship with Dermot: he had smashed up part of the cottage, threatened her and driven off to spend the night with another woman. Sally was frightened. Frightened by Dermot, by what he had done, by what he might do, of losing him. And frightened by the prospect of being alone in the cottage. All this had just happened, over Christmas and the New Year holiday.

After about an hour of telephone conversation, for most of which I had on my counselling hat, we decided that Sally would come to England for a few days and stay with me. It would get her away from a place where she had very recent bad memories, a place where she felt ill at ease, and she could have a completely different environment in which to start to decide what she was going to do.

She flew over in February. St Valentine's Day, ironically enough. We got on well, as usual. She met my youngest daughter, who stayed with me for about 50% of the time. They got on well. After a couple of days Sally and I agreed that I should go and stay with her over the Easter holiday. This was something we could both look forward to.

And that is what happened.

I felt really at home and comfortable during my first ever visit to her cottage. The experience of looking after goats and poultry was new, but felt familiar. When I left we agreed that maybe I could come back in the school summer holiday and spend a bit more time there.

Now it all gets a bit complicated. And intense.

It was only a few weeks later, around the last week in May, when Sally phoned me just after I had got in from work. It was late Friday afternoon, so not a cheap time to be phoning England from Ireland. I don't remember the conversation word for word, but basically she told me that in a few days she was being taken into hospital, completely unexpectedly, with what could prove to be a life-threatening condition. (Throughout my narrative here I am trying to respect Sally's privacy, and being sensitive to personal information. The details do not matter to the story, and I don't want readers to try to guess or read between the lines... that is intrusive and also pointless.)

I was shocked.

After eating I got on to the Internet and did some research. It was all pretty bad news: survival rates were low. If Sally was actually being rushed into hospital then things were about as serious as they could be.

I now had a weekend at home. Madeline, my youngest daughter, was with her mother. I was nearly up to date with marking and paperwork. The time was there for me to use as I wished. And I had no idea as to what to think – my feelings were all over the place; I had no idea what I was going to do.

Over many years I had taught Drama; I had taught English to reluctant adolescents; I had performed on stage; I had written and directed school musicals; I had appeared on live television and on local news programmes. I was used to adrenalin surges and putting myself on the line. I was used to being places where there was nowhere to hide. I had trained and practised as a counsellor and was reasonably self-aware and competent in dealing with emotions and crises. But this felt so different.

In retrospect (often so much easier than recognising what is going on in the present, in the present!), maybe this is where I found an affinity with County Wicklow. Because I found my life moving along in two different, but obviously linked, ways – or levels. Or something like that...

Time was changing internally at a different speed to how it was changing externally. I cannot explain it with words such as osmosis or symbiosis; although those give a bit of a feel for what began.

Here, lying in Don's field, watching the sky and aching pleasantly from physical labour, it all seemed so easy and so far away. Now, I suppose, I was adapted; still learning to adjust, but well on the way to reconciling that once the door had opened and I had gone through, there was no return; so I had better get used to the path I had chosen.

Back then, only a few years ago in time but aeons ago in experience and learning and awareness, I felt battered by events and my instinctive reactions to those events.

On the Saturday morning after Sally's phone call I got in my car and drove to the seaside. If you'll excuse the pun... I felt driven to take a walk along the beach.

I found a parking space behind the town's Pavilion. On the advertising hoardings outside were posters advertising the event for the day – a 'Psychic Fayre'.

I liked to think I had an open mind about such things. My mother had mentioned to me some time ago that she was part of a healing group where she lived in Devon, but I had never asked her much about that. As I have written before, my great-grandfather was a water diviner, or dowser. And I seemed to recall that my grandmother had something to do with being friends with a medium, or holding séances. Or something. Most of which I thought was probably exploitative. So I never enquired. But looking at that poster and feeling what I was feeling and thinking about Sally, I felt I had a better understanding of why it was that people should attend such events and spend their money on... whatever it was on offer there. However, I walked past and, as the tide was low, on to the beach.

I can't say I remember what I was thinking. I don't really remember the walk. But I do remember sitting on a bench on the promenade and smoking a small cigar. I was calm and, I think, outwardly nothing betrayed my thoughts and feelings.

Then a woman came and sat next to me. I remember two things about her: she had long, thick, hennaed hair and she spoke with an Irish accent.

"Are ye alright?" she asked, smiling at me.

I was a little startled but, "Yes, fine thanks."

"Only there's a bit of bother around you. If ye don't mind me saying so..."

What should I say? Or do?

"Can I talk to ye, like? Is that OK?"

"Sure," I said.

"You have some very serious choices to make, don't you?" She didn't wait for an answer. "I can see that. And fair play to you for thinking it through. Because this is life-changing stuff we have here. For the woman and for you. Yeah... for the two of youse now."

I remember deliberately not looking at this woman, this stranger, but staring ahead, out to sea. I think I was afraid that if I looked at her I might break down. I had not a clue who she was... though I could guess from where she came. And I had no idea what she wanted or why she sat to talk with me in this way. I hoped she didn't want any money, as I had none and no intention of paying her for anything. I had come here for peace and quiet, calmness, reflection; this felt like being poked with a stick.

"But let me tell you... it'll be OK. Whatever you do, it'll be OK. She does have xxxxxx, you know that now, don't you? When she goes into hospital that's what they'll find. I'm sorry to shock you like this... but I think you know, don't you?" I nodded. "Of course you know. And you also know what you're gonna do, don't you? Because really you have no choice now, do you?

Because she needs you. There's nobody else, and you will have the power to do what needs to be done. And you will get all the help you need. And not only will you help with the healing, you will get what *you* need too. Because although you think this is for her, it'll also be for you."

On reflection, maybe I was in a state of shock, because I was not fazed by this woman and what she was saying. It all seemed natural and real. True. It had a ring of feeling true.

"You know, my friend," she said, standing up now, "I sort of envy you. You could be about to go on a big adventure. The biggest you can imagine. Or can't imagine, more like. And you will have tough times but also some fantastic. One thing I will say just before I leave you... cos I can tell you have much thinking and much to do. Just remember that you have free will. It's up to you." Then she laughed. "That's the theory, anyway!"

She held out her hand, waiting for me to shake it.

"Good luck, son," she said. (Son? She was younger than I!) "I know you'll do what is right."

I stood and shook her hand. There was a moment of real intensity: a time-stood-still moment when our eyes briefly locked. Then she dropped my hand, turned and headed back towards the Fayre, leaving me to slump back on the seat and stub out the cigar that was, by now, almost burning my fingers.

In a bit of a daze, I found my car and started the drive home, probably still in some sort of state of shock. I replayed the conversation over and over; the journey home seemed a blur.

In fact, the whole evening was a blur: a windswept, foggy landscape of thoughts and feelings that came and went out of my consciousness, rolling through my head, unformed shapes and images that would not focus. I could not be dismissive, yet it had all seemed so unreal. I argued with myself, going round and round... and ending up nowhere.

The next day, Sunday, consisted of a morning of marking children's work, a lunch break and then the usual telephone call to see how my mother was doing. Except this particular Sunday and this particular phone call turned out not to be exactly usual.

My mother had known Sally from the 1960s. She also knew I had seen her recently. But I had to tell my mother the news of Sally's illness. And also maybe use the phone call as an opportunity to share my thoughts and feelings, and possible ways forward. I had yet to decide whether or not to tell her about the mysterious Irish woman at the seaside.

So, the phone call starts off quite normally: a brief exchange of inconsequential stuff like what the weather was like etc. Then I launched in to tell her about Sally phoning me.

It is fortunate that phone calls at the weekend were free for up to an hour. Then you hang up and redial in order to get the next hour free. I redialled twice before we had finished. (Although I write "finished", it was far from finished... and the next two evenings saw further calls between us.)

It did not take long, during that first, Sunday afternoon phone call for something to happen.

As a teacher of English and Drama, as someone who wrote scripts, and as a counsellor, I was used to thinking in metaphor and pictures, as well as words; used to combining what these days is called 'left brain' with 'right brain' thinking. Consequently, when pictures and sounds dropped in to me, I was not concerned I was having a psychotic episode... and I just went with it. My poor mother just had to try to keep up with the novel things that were happening as I told her what I was seeing and hearing. It was like working on several levels... just like when working on a script: living in the here and now but also in the there and then. In some ways this made the whole process easier... or essentially *possible*, even; in other ways I still had to ask myself what was real and what was in my imagination. Something that can still happen, even now...

It was only in retrospect that I realised how I was able to discern when what was happening was genuine: I started to get physical reactions. My arms would tingle or my legs shake when the intensity and focus became greater: basically, I suppose, when I got deeper into whatever was happening. Now and again I would feel I could come up for breath but there seemed to be such a lot that I had to take in, absorb, learn and try to understand.

This is not easy to write about – not because of any sensitivities but because there are not always the words to describe. It is similar to asking somebody to break down, into its component parts, a multimedia collage art-house movie that plays at different speeds on a number of screens simultaneously. And the dialogue is sometimes foreign, the music sometimes cacophonous, the characters a mix of real people and transient figures, the colours dazzling then black and white... However, I'll pick out what I can.

So, I'm telling my mother (Beth) about Sally and my concerns for her well-being. Suddenly my concentration is interrupted by a picture of what appears to be somebody who looks similar to, but I know isn't, my (long dead) grandmother, tending a large allotment. At the same time the breath is almost sucked out of my body and my legs tremble. This is completely unexpected and rather frightening. Am I overstressed? Having a heart attack or a stroke? Yet I don't feel anything except positive. It's like a warm wind of affection flowing through me at the same time as being slapped in the face.

To my mother's credit she not only accepted what was going on, she was not only completely supportive – she positively helped and pushed or carried me as I went along this new road.

I told her what I was seeing. Maybe she, too, tuned in. I don't know, but she asked me for more detail. I gave it to her. She told me to ask – whoever this woman was – who they were. So I did. (I do not recall how much of what I said I actually spoke and how much was in my head: it was a mix of being in two worlds at once... like channel-hopping on the television. But at least some of what I said must have been aloud because my mother was able to help with prompts.)

After an indeterminate amount of time it became clear that the woman I was seeing was somebody known to my mother: an old friend of *her* mother's, my grandmother. It was somebody known to us as Mrs B. Mrs B used to live in the same road as us; she and her husband ran a flower shop in Bristol, stocked largely from their own market garden on the outskirts of the city. However, what was especially relevant to my present experience was that Mr B and my grandmother used to hold séances where Mrs B acted as a medium. What I was seeing was the dead Mrs B who was coming through to me, for some reason.

As I focussed in on the pictures I saw a greenhouse; coming out of the greenhouse was a man in an old trilby and a light brown three-quarter length coat. He smiles at me and Mrs B introduces me to him. She told me his name was Dan and he was there to help me. She then faded away.

Dan and I sat together on a garden bench in the market garden, looking at a stream a few feet away. We just sit there doing nothing, while pictures continue to come to me. I think that Dan was a facilitator of some sort. Maybe a guide; I still don't know for sure what his roles were/are. But he seemed to link the worlds I was jumping between. He stayed with me – or rather was available to me – for several years. I can still access, or meet with, Dan should I feel the need or want.

Among the pictures I saw was a tree. This tree was the shape of an oak, but instead of leaves there were bits of paper all over the branches. I also saw a large lake – then two – set in some hills. Between the hills there appeared the logo from the National Lottery (the hand with fingers crossed). Slowly the fingers uncross and start to beckon me onwards.

I also heard lots of chattering, but the words were unclear; it was like being in a room next to another room where there was a big meeting going on.

Somehow I knew that I had to make a journey: literal as well as metaphorical. Indeed, the two were part of the same whole.

Eventually I told my mother that I thought all this meant I had to go to Ireland to be with Sally, though I wasn't sure what I could do; or if, indeed, I'd be welcome. Or if it would be possible. What about my job? My house? My family?

In the meantime, Sally was seriously ill.

My mother told me about the Harry Edwards Healing Sanctuary. Later I looked them up on the Internet. I followed their advice and wrote a letter requesting help (healing) for Sally. I also sent them a donation. A few weeks later I had a letter from them saying they were aware that Sally was now out of hospital and the operation had gone well. But they would continue to send healing. This was news to me. I wasn't even aware at the time the letter arrived that Sally had had her operation.

Back to the phone calls with my mother that last weekend in May: I had some extremely serious decisions to make. Life-changing ones. But I felt that if I jumped off the cliff into the abyss of the drastic and unknown, I would be caught and held. I suppose I was facing a leap of faith! Yet I had no time in which to work out what the faith was in… what I believed was going on.

As it happened I didn't need the time.

When I went into school on the Monday morning I must have looked wrecked. I didn't feel it but one of my colleagues… friends… a Deputy Head, took me into his office and asked me if I was OK. He and I had worked for several years doing counselling work with students and staff.

I told him of my concerns for Sally – but nothing of the phone calls and my dilemma. He volunteered that he had had a close friend of his die of the same disease that Sally had, and if I wanted to leave my job it would not be a problem, even though the date for resignation for that term had passed. They would find ways around it all. If I felt that I had to go to Ireland (his idea, not mine!) then they would do all they could to help. He reminded me of the woman I had employed as a counselling supervisor for the staff counsellors, and suggested I talk with her.

I knew that Hilda (the supervisor) didn't take on new clients but called her anyway. She was happy to help, so I arranged some sessions with her to talk through what I would do. I also called an estate agent to come and value my house. Just in case.

There is no need to go into the details. Suffice it to say that a month later, by the end of June, I was on the ferry to Ireland, my house sold, the money in the bank, my job gone and agreements made with Madeline and her mother that this was OK and that I would, as soon as sensible, organise a trip for Madeline to visit me in Ireland. All I told Sally was that I was coming to look after her during her convalescence. I really don't like the phrase, "It was meant to happen" – but I was amazed at how smoothly and easily (luckily? Now there's a discussion to be had..!) everything went.

So here I was now, a couple of years later, lying in an Irish field with such a lot of high-energy events behind me.

Before moving on to the rest of the day, I'll briefly go back a few paragraphs to: "I also saw a large lake – or two – set in some hills. Between the hills there appeared the logo from the National Lottery (the hand with fingers crossed)."

A few months into Sally's recovery she felt well enough to take me to some of the local attractions. One of them was Glendalough... a place of spiritual pilgrimage for many Catholics. We parked the car, walked along the path, through the woods and arrived at the main loch. I was completely taken aback. Standing on the beach of the lake I took in the view... it was the one I had been shown during the telephone call with my mother; however, there was no National Lottery logo between the hills!

By this time I was becoming used to what some may consider strange goings-on, coincidences, synchronicities etc; nevertheless it gave me the shivers. I had never heard of Glendalough nor, as far as I knew, ever seen pictures.

So when I heard laughter coming from the field boundary, between the bushes, I didn't feel spooked or even especially surprised. I had learned, I hope, to respect and cherish the unusual: maybe even embrace it as my new normality. It wasn't intrusive; it just was what it was. I had accepted the feelings of being connected to place, to animals and something other. I had, as I write about later, experienced more episodes of mediumship; contact with what may have been an angel; elements of shamanism; learned something about the Kabbalah; absent healing of people; precognition... so what was a bit of laughter?

I only had a few more posts to erect in this part of Don's farm. I collected my tools and walked along the final boundary hedge. As I did so the movements through the bushes and saplings moved just ahead of me... as did the chuckles. I worked on, ignoring all of this, doing the digging and sinking the posts until I got to the last post-hole to be dug.

I was now on the edge of the farmland, the fern-covered moorland/hillside beyond. Something made me pause before thrusting the pickaxe into the ground. Instead I scrabbled at the bottom of the grassy bank with my hands. I have no idea why. Suddenly, behind me, I heard the raucous "caw" of a crow, or rook... my bird-recognition skills are not great. There, hopping around in the field was a large black bird... not more than six feet away from me. I hadn't heard it land, nor seen it flying around. Before I knew it there were another two of these birds, landing alongside the first. They all seemed oblivious of me, yet obviously knew I was there. I suppose they had a certain arrogance, or sense of belonging, that was not going to be ruffled by my presence.

All three hopped to a place about three feet away from where I was planning to dig. They all pecked the ground and then took off. I felt, as well as heard, their wings beating through the air. At the same time the chuckles I had been hearing suddenly went silent; it was one of those occasions when I was conscious of the sound only when it had stopped.

I looked around. I was alone. It was silent. No laughter, no birds, no sound of sheep or of cattle, or of wind.

I went to the spot where the black birds had pecked, and pushed the spade into the ground. It gave way; this was somewhat unusual as most of the previous digging had involved actively persuading stones and rocks out of the way.

I started to make a hole. The soil continued to be accommodating in its pliability and consistency. After about six inches I decided to use my hands. I knelt down and, like a dog *unburying* a bone, threw the dirt out of the hole with both hands.

Within a few minutes I had hit something. I slowed down but continued to pull out sods, the occasional root and small stones.

I peered into the hole: not much to see. I became more archaeological in my digging, taking it quite gently and spreading the area of my excavations. Eventually I uncovered a large black slab. I increased the size of the hole. The slab was smooth and shiny, several feet across... and I still couldn't find the edges. It was buried in the hole at an angle of about 45 degrees.

I brushed off the remaining crumbs of dirt, sat back and looked at it.

To this day I have no idea what it was: marble, onyx, granite... natural or artificial... but I know that it was huge and covering something. I also knew that I had to leave it there. It seemed silly. I had uncovered something fascinating and maybe intriguing, but I could go no further. I could not find the edges; it would have been wrong to try to force it up and out with the wrecking bar, pickaxe... whatever. I could have got Don to come with the tractor and ask him to lift it. But having found it, it had to be reburied and left.

So I backfilled the hole; but as I did so I stuffed it full of rocks, large stones... anything I could find close by that might dissuade someone in the future to bother with it.

I then moved a few feet away and completed my fencing posts.

As I walked away from the field, dragging the tools I had been using all day, I heard rustling from the boundaries, and a quiet chatter. I saw nothing. But I knew I had done the right thing and that I would not disclose my discovery.

As I neared the gate at the opposite end of the field I turned around to look at my handiwork. On top of the final post, the one close to the mysterious slab, sat an owl. As I watched, it flapped its wings and took off into the nearby copse.

I dropped the spade, bar and axe and watched it fly away. As I did so, staring hard to watch, I became almost hypnotised by its flight.

Then two things happened. One: I found myself thinking that I hadn't seen many, if any, birds of prey since arriving in Wicklow. Two: I saw, in my head, a hawk of some sort. As I saw the hawk I felt pulled towards it. I let go of my thoughts and… this is so difficult to describe… I actually found myself being that hawk. I was, somehow, inside it. I was seeing what it was seeing. And what it was seeing was someone I knew.

When teaching in my last school I had had a friend and colleague, Connie, who taught French. We had kept in touch for a while after I'd left: one of the few members of staff with whom I had remained in contact. She recently had resigned her job and moved to France to live permanently, working in a château for a family. As I looked down, from inside the hawk, I saw Connie way below me walking across a courtyard and carrying a tray with glasses and a bottle of wine.

I have no idea how long this incident lasted. It was a fleeting glimpse but felt like many minutes. Perhaps the shock of what had happened distorted my perceptions, but I snapped out of it and found myself back on the farm. However, I now sensed, in a Rupert Sheldrake sort of way, I suppose, that I was not alone in the field. I felt as if I had a hawk sitting on my left shoulder. Not only that, on the ground beside me I felt a toad. Or frog. I think that even at that time... and certainly now... it would be better described as having Hawk on my shoulder and Toad beside me. Because what I believe I was experiencing was what shamans might call power animals and totem animals. More of which later.

I returned to the farmhouse, reported that I'd completed my task for the day and drove back to the cottage; I felt a sense of amusement, awe and wondering what would happen next. What an experience all this was!

Chapter Six

This is the final chapter of this book. There are anecdotes here that haven't really fitted elsewhere; there are some loose ends tied up; there are some reflections on what all this may have meant, both then and now.

But before getting into bits and pieces, I link to the end of the previous chapter.

I left the Crowne farm feeling elated, disappointed and confused. I had not helped with their calf and that was disappointing. Maybe it was more a blow to my Ego than anything else: another reminder to keep everything in perspective and to find the line between questioning and accepting. The incidents in the field where I had been sinking fence posts left me quite elated; I still felt a bit of a buzz. The hawk and frog/toad required some thought, or meditations, though I sensed I knew what this was all about.

The cottage was empty when I got home. I immediately emailed Connie to tell her about the hawk incident. It didn't take long for her to reply. She confirmed that she had been in the courtyard at that time, she had been carrying a tray with wine and glasses, and that she had seen a hawk flying overhead.

Sally's shift pattern meant she wouldn't be back for some hours. I had a shower, changed into some clean clothes, made some tea and went through to sit in the end room, overlooking the paddock.

As I prepared to sit and drink my tea, I looked out of the large patio doors. The hens and the ducks were all together, in a small tight group, as far from the road as they could get. This was very unusual. They were also quite quiet… not silent but no kerfuffle or calling. Often the ducks would be in and out of the stream and the hens would be pecking about anywhere between the animal houses close to the road and the paddock fencing next to the Big

Meadow. The only creature near the animal houses was Circe, who was walking around her house and the henhouses and past the duck house. She was then pausing, looking up at the birds, and continuing to circle the lower end of the paddock. She did this several times while I watched. It was like she was on patrol.

I continued to watch, fascinated; it was all rather strange and I couldn't understand what was happening. Then the birds seemed to get fed up. As if with one single mind, they began to disperse from the group and spread out, down the slope, behaving normally again. Circe saw this and moved towards them. In the way that she helped sometimes when we were putting the poultry away at night, she began to manoeuvre so that she cut off any birds heading towards the middle of the paddock, and her movements pushed the birds back in the corner. Noise filtered through the patio doors: Circe whinnying and the birds complaining. The poultry were being shepherded by the goat so that they were contained again in a small group.

I turned the key in the lock and pulled up the handle, ready to go out and either investigate or stop this nonsense. Circe had never shown animosity or bullying tendencies towards the birds before, but something must have upset her for her to behave in such a forceful way. She marched up and down in front of the birds, effectively preventing them from going anywhere.

As the hens and ducks again became resigned to being cornered, Circe looked around and back at the duck house, where the stream poured into the ditch by the road. Suddenly she rushed across the paddock, leaving her patrolling duties in a mad dash of energetic mania.

At this point I opened the door, quite concerned for the goat's welfare. I wondered if she'd been stung, perhaps. The birds remained where they were, almost transfixed. But Circe was pawing at the edge of the stream, head down, and front legs kicking up the dirt and grass. Then she stood on her back legs and stamped down with her front ones. Several times she reared up and thumped down. It was forceful and almost vicious.

I got to the paddock gate and climbed on to it. As I did so I was able to see from a greater height; and what I saw was that in front of Circe, cowering in the stream, lay a creature that I did not immediately recognise. Then I understood. Circe was keeping at bay a mink. She was protecting the birds and trying to see off the intruder that she knew was a likely predator of the hens and ducks.

I sat astride the gate thinking about what to do. I was glad that Sally's children were not there because they'd have rushed to the gun cabinet and vied to be the one to shoot the mink. Circe seemed to have the situation under control, but it was hardly fair to expect a goat to take responsibility for the safety of the birds. I could rush across, shouting; I could sit and watch; I could ask Cernunnos for help again. None of these felt quite right. So I eased off the gate and slid down the gate into the paddock. The birds all stood still and Circe reverted to her pawing of the ground.

I couldn't see into the stream from where I was now, so I walked quickly, but, I hoped, stealthily, upstream of where Circe and the mink were facing off. As I got closer I could see the mink still on the edge of the stream, still hunched down... obviously scared but uncertain what to do, completely still. Circe continued to rear up and stamp down at frequent intervals. I was between them and the birds, which I hoped would now be safe. In contrast to the tensions in and around the paddock, the water in the stream was making its trickling-over-the-stones music.

I now walked slowly, following the stream from the Big Meadow fencing towards the mink. It saw me. Circe saw me... and whinnied. I clicked my tongue at her, making a noise but not articulating words. I hoped it was a reassuring noise for her.

I called Circe and she was obviously conflicted. However, eventually she turned away from the stream and looked at me, although still remaining on her guard. The mink seemed to wake up. It turned and flashed away, its body lithe and athletic.

I ran down the paddock, looking to see if I could trace where it had got in and got out. I just caught a flash of movement in the ditch alongside the road. It had either climbed the tree and jumped down, or squeezed under the sheep fencing; it mattered not, because it was gone.

Circe and I stood for a few seconds, looking at one another. I walked over to her; she was shaking. I leaned down and put my arms around her neck, giving her a cuddle. I then scratched the top of her head and under her chin... something I knew she found sybaritic. I knelt there, whispering reassurances, congratulations and thanks to her, until she stopped shaking. She pulled away and wandered off into her own shed, where she lay down on her straw bed... but from where she could look out of the door at the paddock in front of her.

The birds, meanwhile, had resumed their usual activity; maybe oblivious to the lucky escape they had had.

I inspected the whole paddock, checking for carcasses and bloodied feathers, just in case I'd arrived too late, but all was well. So I went back indoors and sat, drinking my tea with the patio door open, listening to the birds now safely pecking away in the paddock or splashing in the stream.

In some ways I was disappointed. I had hoped that all the livestock would be safe, protected by Cernunnos. On the other hand, the livestock *was* safe: saved by the goat! Maybe Cernunnos *had* helped, using Circe as a vehicle/conduit. Then I realised that maybe all I had done with the boundary-walking was ask for protection from foxes. I had no doubts that had worked. It was, maybe, my lack of foresight or narrow vision which had allowed the mink on to our land.

It would do no harm, and maybe it would work again – I had to call on Cernunnos to help protect the birds, and goat, from any predators. I would walk the boundary and ask for assistance.

As I stood up to take my now empty mug into the kitchen I

felt that something had shifted again. I was unclear as to what it was, but as I called Cernunnos to mind, the thoughts were somehow fresher and clearer than I expected. He was no longer at a distance to be called upon, he was right there, right next to me. There would be no need for meditation or working hard at calling him: he'd be there.

Also at this point I suddenly understood why frog/toad was with me.

At one point on the drive back from the Crownes I had wondered if I was being told something about the way the ducks greedily harvested the frog/toad population from the stream. It was quite common to see a duck waddling triumphantly from one part of the stream, with a struggling amphibian in its beak. Now I began to realise that I was back into metaphors. But just what was it that was being represented?

Duh! Stupid. Amphibians lived happily in water and on land; they were comfortable in two worlds. I was also living in two worlds: one being, for want of a better phrase, the material world, the other the world of spirit. And in the latter there were many sub-worlds, some of which I was beginning to discover.

When all this began in earnest, a few years previously when I was living in England, I was quite happily living in the world of air and earth. I had had a few excursions into the world of water (spirit) but not much more than excursions. Now, however, I was finding that being thrown in at the deep end had enabled me to swim, including swimming underwater.

This leads me into another story: one that took place some time after I had moved to Ireland.

I had travelled back to the UK to visit friends and family. Up until this point I had had no spiritual connections with anyone from my previous life, and certainly not with people I had never met before.

I knew little about Pamela when we were introduced by Beth, my mother, who knew Pamela quite well. She was a little older than I; her husband was dead and Beth told me that she was spiritually aware, but I knew few details.

After the initial social niceties we sat and had a chat about matters spiritual: exchanging experiences in a cautious but matter-of-fact way. With strangers I have always found it wise to be cautious when talking about these things... it is easy to offend, overwhelm, bamboozle, bore or generally upset. However, we seemed to be getting on well.

Suddenly I got one of my physical reactions: the arm tingle and twitch. I knew this signified some sort of connection. Even more suddenly I was completely awash with emotion. It was like somebody had opened the top of my head and poured in a cocktail of intense feelings. In some ways it was embarrassing... here I was as a guest in a stranger's home shaking and gasping and gulping for air. But Pamela just looked at me and said, "It's OK. Go on."

Ten minutes later I had delivered messages from her husband in spirit. I had relived his death in front of her... the first time I had ever been so clairsentient... and reassured her that he was fine. (This has always struck me as odd. Someone dead telling their living loved one that they are "fine" or "OK" or "well"... but we are just the messenger!) It was a draining yet exhilarating experience. I realised later that the reason for such a strong physical reaction – I thought they were a thing of the past by this time – was that Pamela was a stranger and I had no other connection with her dead husband. Previous readings I had given were for friends or family... so connections already existed. I presume her husband had to ensure I knew what was happening and make a huge effort to get through. He also did not know me so the amount of energy he had to use would have been an unknown. I guess he put more into it than I was comfortable with! However, it taught me what the limits were for me: a necessary lesson in order to be able to take charge – we are never asked to do more than we can manage. It also confirmed that what I was doing was real. I didn't know Pamela; with friends and family readings there was always the doubt about whether I was imagining things or using memories.

There was no sense of time during this, and I had few memories of what I had said to Pamela; I just hoped it was what she wanted and needed. No worries. She was thrilled, and, apparently, not in the least bit surprised.

Over the next few hours we all had a long talk. I learned some important things as a result: the physical reactions were unnecessary but a way that spirit (or my guide/s, to be specific) found to help me realise that it was not just my imagination but an actual phenomenon that I was experiencing; I was always in charge and if I didn't like/want what was happening I could ask for it to stop; always, always, always give the message as I hear/see it: it might seem nonsense or silly to me... but that doesn't mean it is to whoever is receiving it; keep the white light of protection switched on; the chances are that I would connect with those with whom I had something in common. Just as the famous American medium John Edward connects with those who have worked in medical care, just as he did, I would tune in more easily to those who were educators, or to adolescents... which was the age group I had spent years teaching. Or people who had something in common with me. Pamela's husband had loved boats and the water... just as I did. Pamela also reassured me (role reversal here?!) that my fretting about whether or not to "be a medium" or to "be a healer" or "study shamanism" was redundant: I could *do* all of those... *be* a generalist and not a specialist... be myself.

Another example of 'if you don't understand the message, keep going' was earlier on in my stay in Ireland.

I was still in the habit of phoning my mother every Sunday evening. Sometimes we would exchange news; sometimes we would have a visitor from spirit try to join us. There is one incident that taught me several things... not only about being persistent, but also the use of metaphor.

Towards the end of this particular telephone conversation I was aware that somebody was trying to connect through me. I told my mother so that she could help by boosting the energies. I also felt that it was someone she once knew. However, the picture I was being shown was odd.

The house we lived in when I was a child had a coal-hole. I was seeing somebody delivering sacks of coal to that house. My first thought was that my mother knew the man delivering. I told her what I was seeing but neither of us could understand it. She had no idea who it was and I was getting more frustrated. I kept asking, "Who are you?" and the same picture was broadcast in my head: a man delivering coal to our old house. We considered if it was one of our old neighbours trying to get attention. No. The picture remained. We considered all sorts, speculating in ever increasing bizarre ways.

Suddenly the delivery stopped. All that was left was a pile of coal. All this time I was describing to my mother the scene as I saw it. Two bits of coal came into focus. I said to my mother, "It's just coals." This was when she had her 'Aha' moment.

It was nothing to do with the delivery. Nothing to do with the man. It was her old friend whose name was Joy Coles.

Once we had 'got it' Joy was able to pass on all sorts. Subsequently, Joy has connected several times: it seems that once we were tuned in to her, she could make herself known without the need for metaphor or pun.

This use of metaphor also sometimes infiltrates into my meditations. In some ways it is very useful (provided I am not being too dense to understand it!); in other ways it can add to confusion about what is real, what is imagination, what is metaphor... The only way to sort this out, for me, has been practice.

I have found that once I have had a particular spirit experience it gets easier to have another similar experience, and it is possible to learn from and build upon these experiences. There was only one time when an experience I had was unique.

Again it was while talking during a Sunday phone call to my mother. We were discussing the notion that one of the reasons for being in Ireland was possibly unfinished business with Sally. It occurred to me that maybe one of the underlying themes within this unfinished business was that of loyalty. As I mentioned the word something happened within me. I could use the word 'transported' or the phrase 'a different dimension' – it was similar to the hawk experience, but this time I was another person. I was a young girl in a farmhouse kitchen in France several hundred years ago. It was the time of the French Revolution. I have no idea how I knew this, but I just did. I knew.

Soldiers burst in through the door, scaring me and demanding to know where my father was. I wouldn't tell them. They attacked me and dragged me outside.

As all this was happening to me I was describing it to my mother. When the narrative completed I was back to being myself. My mother said, "Wow, what was that all about?"

"I thought I was telling you as it went along."

"You were. But it was all in a foreign language. It sounded like French to me. But old fashioned, if you know what I mean."

I had studied French at 'A' level so was not a complete novice with the language… but it had been years since I had spoken it. My assumption was, and still is, that I was experiencing something from a past life. This may explain why I feel an affinity to France and things French. I feel comfortable there. It is also interesting that one of my children chose to live there. However, maybe that's all imagination?!

Another one-off experience that I have deliberately chosen not to try to repeat involved one of my work colleagues.

After a year or so of living in Ireland, and with Sally well on the mend, I found myself employment at a school. One of my colleagues was Bridget. We got on well and worked closely together. One of the things we did together was home-school visits, so we would be out on the road touring the catchment area. This meant time in the car; sometimes meeting parents and children in somewhat of an emotional state; sharing anecdotes and experiences from each of our cultures and backgrounds and, as time went on and we became good friends, occasionally I would tune in to her dead relatives and friends. I would give her readings.

One day Bridget was not in school. Nobody had heard from her; she had not phoned in sick. This was unusual for her. To say I was worried would be an exaggeration; however, I did wonder what the story was.

As I was wondering – daydreaming basically – I found myself looking around a bedroom. Bridget was in the bed, asleep. I could see the wardrobe with her clothes inside, the curtains drawn at the window, the soft toys on the bed and on a chair close by. I could make out the colours and pattern on the carpet.

Although I was initially fascinated, I knew this was wrong. Whatever had happened, I should not be doing it. This was intrusive. I put a block on it. A few years later I learned that what I had done was 'remote viewing', but I had done it unconsciously.

When Bridget returned to work I told her what had happened, having spent some time weighing up the reasons why I should or should not tell her. She confirmed the details of what I had seen. I felt a mixture of triumph and dread. What a thing to be able to do… but the responsibilities coming from this ability were beyond what I wanted right then. Or now. So I never have tried to replicate it. Another example of always being in charge.

It must be said, though, that "being in charge" does not mean getting what you want or expect. What it does mean is that it is possible to opt out of what is happening, especially if it is making you feel uneasy in some way. Just because you *can* doesn't mean you *must* or *should*. I will write something more about this when commenting on Ego matters.

Next, two accounts of healing involving people:

I went to Ireland because Sally was ill. The hospital had done what they had to do but she was still ill upon her return home. My experience of healing was extremely limited; basically it consisted of what I had read (which was extensive), listening to healers talk and attending various workshops. The one I remember most was when I was sat in the circle and receiving healing myself but suddenly found that I was giving more healing back to the person (an experienced practitioner) who was healing me. I had also used my regular meditations to try giving absent healing.

I had been in Ireland a few weeks and was getting into a routine. It must have been highly disruptive for Sally, who was not expecting this, but we managed the situation pretty well.

One night I woke in the middle of the night. This was before Sally went back to work, so she was also in bed.

I turned on to my back and became aware of tingling feelings all over me. As I watched, a huge glowing light emerged out of the darkness just beyond the bottom of our bed and formed something like a pillar, changing from white to gold in colour. Sally remained asleep. Out of the light reached a hand and I was passed a box containing a crystal. It wasn't a box that was solid, it wasn't materialised, but I knew that I was being handed something very precious in an extraordinary way. I suppose I should have been frightened, but I wasn't. I also knew – I have no idea how – that this was a gift from the Archangel Raphael. I don't suppose it was Raphael himself who was there in our bedroom, I presume it was an emissary, but it was a powerful and awe-inspiring presence. I knew that I had to place this box on Sally's stomach and it would morph its way inside her; once there it would move where required in her body, complete her healing and protect her in the future. So this is what I did, giving thanks while I did so.

This was not fantasy, nor a dream. Quite why we were given this gift I have no idea. But what a blessing it was.

The following morning Sally awoke saying she felt good and she would look for work very soon. I did not tell her of the night's proceedings; I'm not sure why. I suppose there's an ethical dilemma here, but I chose to remain silent on the subject. Although Sally was accepting of the things that had been going on, saying she would support me by being the grounding factor, it seemed unfair to tell her: more pressure on her, perhaps. I don't know. But by now I was learning to trust my instincts, and instincts told me to say nothing.

A much later example of trusting when involved with a healing was after I had left Ireland.

I used to send distant healing to a number of people. One day I learned that an older relative of mine, Ron, was dying from cancer. He had been admitted to hospital and was not expected to leave. He was not somebody I knew very well, having only met him on a few occasions. Nevertheless he was family, and I felt some sort of connection with him.

I decided to spend most of one meditation on Ron alone. Usually I spent the half hour or so sending healing to a number of different people. I would then keep topping it up between meditations. But this time I wanted to concentrate on one person. I had no idea what I was going to do: a question of 'Let go and let God', I suppose; but I sat down and made my preparations.

When sending healing I take myself to a special place in my mind: a sort of pastoral idyll picture with a healing pool, waterfall, woodland etc. It is a place I find peaceful and harmonious. I then have a ritual as part of my meditation whereby I visualise the people to whom I want healing sent; they are part of the picture and if I have their consent (in spirit), we can proceed with whatever is appropriate for them.

With Ron it was different. There was a blockage there and I just couldn't picture him in the middle of the scene... which is where other people started from.

At first I thought it was some sort of failure on my part: I was unable to connect; he wouldn't give permission; my intent was somehow tarnished; I was having an off day... whatever. I gave up, ready to try another day.

When I tried again I realised that my expectation was in the way; maybe there was still too much of my Ego involved. I let go, again, and as I did so became aware of Ron hovering in a corner. He was on the edge of my picture, in a part I hadn't really noticed much. It was a high rocky path that looked down on the rest of the scene. Ron was there.

As I saw him we connected and I knew that he wasn't there for the healing of his illness or the easing of his pain; he was there because he was frightened of dying. The healing that he required was to be reassured. Like a small boy going to the dentist for the first time, perhaps. My job was to help assuage his fears.

I tried to send him as much Universal Love as I could. As I did so a party of four pairs of men, all dressed in white robes, carried a sort of pallet, or portable bed, from behind Ron and up the path. As they walked away from the edge of the picture I could see that Ron was on the bed they were carrying. I felt that he knew who all these people were and was deriving great comfort from this. I had no idea what was going on. I had not invited this procession into my picture, though I was happy to see them there, and I had no idea who they were, or what they were doing.

I trusted in what was going on and left them to it.

A few days later, when meditating for him once more, the scene was almost repeated. Almost. This time he was not hovering, frightened, in the corner: he was already on the pallet and the procession continued up the path.

Whenever I did the topping up for Ron I had a glimpse of this procession. He was protected, he was being carried, he was less fearful. Some weeks later he died. I gather from his wife that she felt he had died in peace; this is also what I felt.

For me this is a classic example of the Universe doing what is necessary; of course, the question is, did I help or would this have happened anyway?

Which brings me neatly on to the issue of Ego: because Ego and its relationship with the All/Everything/Multiverse – whatever you want to call it – is central.

Many books and theses have been written about the nature of the Ego – including its relationship with spiritual growth and understanding. All I can do is comment from my own experience and hope that this helps makes sense of something that confronts and often confuses us. (I intentionally write "us" because I do not exclude myself from being confused!) Looking at the subject will also involve a brief consideration of what might be meant by karma, destiny, fate, free will, 'meaning', love and being human. I shall not be writing a logical, empirically based argument in any great detail, so there will be assertions which could be challenged. That's fine. The process of challenging involves thinking about these things. I defy anybody to prove that what I write is either 100% right or 100% wrong for everybody. We are all different and have different experiences. Theories are theories, that is all.

So that's where to start. Ego is what separates us from one another… because it is what makes us individuals and aware of our individuality. It is a paradox. Because we are self-aware we recognise our essential aloneness and individuality, but this awareness can also recognise that we are all connected; how can we see we are alone unless we see others, too? There can be no concept of aloneness without others being available to highlight that we are alone. Similarly, we must have a well-developed and strong Ego (sense of self and self-awareness) in order to be able to temporarily set it aside. I have heard it said that we must have no Ego in order to be effective 'Lightworkers': the argument seems to be that you cannot be spiritual if you have an Ego.

We are human beings. We are here, alive on this planet, in

order to live our lives. We are spiritual beings trying to be human, not human beings trying to be better spirits. Our Egos can get in the way, which is why they must be well-developed. It is only when the Ego is well-developed that we can set it aside. When the Ego is firm and solid it is possible to move it; when the Ego is weak it tends to flop about all over the place.

It is Buddhists who teach us about being too attached to something, or someone, bringing suffering. Perhaps this attachment is due, in part, to the struggle of the Ego for dominance. If we can (temporarily) detach our Ego we can then become more connected. But our Ego also protects us; so it is not something that can or should be done lightly.

As a counsellor, to connect with my clients, I was taught and practised empathy, being non-judgmental and compassionate. And we tend to think of these as essential to the make-up of a warm, well-balanced, secure, strong human being. I challenge this: it doesn't go far enough.

We talk about tolerance (which, to me, suggests a reluctance – to 'put up with' something) or maybe even 'respect' ("I don't agree with you, but I put up with your right to think/feel/act that way… if you'll do the same for me"). There are hints of a kind of moral superiority behind some of these notions.

For me the greatest, and sometimes most difficult, thing we can give another human being is not compassion, tolerance, respect: it is total acceptance. It is being dispassionate, not compassionate. Or, maybe, to be dispassionately compassionate. It is Universal or Unconditional Love… of someone as an equal. (Dealing with animals and plants is only slightly different; again, reference to Ego within humans.) It is an implicit understanding that we are all doing the best we can; we all have our own struggles, our own ups and downs; we each have a different journey that we must undertake, different lessons to learn and our fellow travellers may be with us at any particular point, then they may divert to go their own path. William Blake sums it all up when he writes, "Everything that lives is holy." The Quakers' (among others) core belief is that there is a spark of the divine within each of us. We may feel that we all are separate, but ultimately we are all part of the Whole and striving to return there.

It is a privilege to be able to have a material body; it allows us to experience so much more than if we were ethereal. But it is only a temporary state.

Ego can make us feel that we are the centre of the Universe. Hence, for example, the prevalence of magical thinking or of superstitions: if I walk on the cracks in the pavement something terrible will happen. If I blaspheme I will be struck by lightning. If I am 'good' then I will be rewarded by some beneficent being. Each of us is part of the Whole, so equally important to the well-being of every other part of the Whole. Reward or punishment *by* the Whole is reward or punishment *of* the Whole.

Because our Ego is in part both a repository for, and a filter of, our feelings, thoughts, memories and experiences, it is largely culturally dependent; after all, we are what we are/who we are because of the culture around us... and vice versa. (And that's culture in a national, ethnic and local sense.) We may feel lost when experiencing another culture: many of the familiarities are missing. It is useful to recognise this because there is a growing tendency, as the world gets smaller and communications across the globe more effective, at least mechanistically, to seek out 'meaning' in other cultures. Hence the spread of Eastern practices such as yoga or meditation into the West; the widespread use of notions such as karma, chakras or the Kabbalah across the world.

If we think of these as spiritual foodstuffs and extend the metaphor: it is good to have a varied diet. We are fortunate to live in an age and place where we can try what, for us, are exotic foods, imported from far away. Some may become a regular part of our lives (curry, for example?). But we are each rooted in the time and place where we were born and grew up. Our physical bodies are tuned to certain foods and drinks. Too much of the unfamiliar and we can become sick... our bodies are not fully acceptant of the change.

I am not saying that we should not try these things; we all have much to learn from, about, other ways of looking at the world, ourselves, one another, Life etc. But seeking too far beyond is usually a fool's errand.

And when we drill down into the basics, most cultures have similar values. We have many more similarities than we have differences. So why is it that so many people seek meaning in cultures other than their own? I can think of several possibilities but am not going to explore them here.

What is fundamental is the persistent quest for meaning that we all seem to have. The ubiquitous 'Why?' question. This is something that crosses cultural boundaries. And I would argue that no culture has all the answers but every culture contributes something to some of the answers. Looking for *the* answer is seeking the Holy Grail; seeking *an* answer or *some of* the answers is the best that can be hoped for. Why? Because nobody can ever have all the answers, yet Ego may drive us to try.

The irony is that by actively trying we are effectively preventing ourselves from finding. Because we are limited by Ego.

But Ego is not a barrier to making progress: it is more of an anchor that keeps us safe; it allows us to make sense of the world as we find it. It protects us. Imagine what it would be like if all the connections across all living things across all of time were permanently open and available. The best metaphor I can find for this is that of a radio being tuned to every station that's broadcasting now, has ever broadcast and will ever broadcast, all at the same time. As material human beings we are too small to be able to deal with this. Our Ego helps us stay tuned in to what we need in the here and now.

As everything is connected and everything is energy, we need Ego to modulate the vibrations of that energy so we can be selective about what we perceive. Because we have free will, there are choices we can make within the connections and energies. However, to continue the radio metaphor, if we normally tune in to AM and want to sometimes go to FM, or vice versa, we need to move the switch. This is where meditation can be helpful.

We can tune in to other stations only when we have tuned out of the one to which we normally listen. Eventually we can learn to use the 'saved station' buttons, and switch quickly between one station and another, even if they are broadcasting on different wavebands.

Our determination to find meaning can also lead to more of what psychologists call an "external locus of control". We come to a belief, maybe permanent, maybe temporary, that we are less able to take control of our lives and they are more controlled by outside forces. Sometimes those forces are other people or situations, sometimes we call them "destiny" or "fate". It is a sneaky way of Ego shifting responsibility.

Logic says we have Free Will, otherwise what's the point? If our Will is sideswiped or just sidetracked, we can dump blame elsewhere. But because we are all connected the knots of those connections and the very complexity of them means that we can never really get to know what the right way is for each of us. And if we throw karma into the mix, and karma is a concept that is not exclusively Eastern but also appears in Christianity, it gets even more bewildering.

Where is all this brain-meandering leading?!

Rudolf Steiner has much to say on many of these issues. One of his concepts that I like is that of mind-knowledge (which would be my speculations in the previous few pages here) and heart-knowledge.

We live in an intellectualised world. We are an evolving

species. There are ancient esoteric arguments that suggest we started as spirit and have, over generations, solidified into the material beings in the material world in which we now find ourselves. We are evolving back towards spirit. This will take many hundreds of thousands of years. But we are where we are and in the time that we are in.

If we don't like the world as it is we have the ability to change it. We all know that love is an overused word ("I'd love a cup of coffee" being very different to "I love my children/parents" to "Love makes the world go around" to "God is Love"). But if we can learn to love our selves, our Selves; if we can learn to really know who we are as individuals and then learn to set Ego aside when appropriate; if we can embrace what makes us different from one another, from animals, from plants, yet still see that everything that lives is, indeed, holy; if we can show each other dispassionate compassion; if we can balance going with the flow of energy from the Universe with taking responsibility for our thoughts, words and actions; if we can cherish what we have more than envy others for what they have and we do not; if we can turn down the intensity so that we can listen to what the Universe is telling us... wow! If, if if... But we can make a start. We can do our bit. And in so doing we celebrate our Self, each other and the world in which we chose to live. That is the way to love. And Love.

I no longer live in Ireland. I no longer have a relationship with Sally. It seems that everything that happened was transitory in some ways; but had a permanent impact on us both.

Although I am certain that I was sent there in order to help heal Sally, I also benefited long term from the experiences I had whilst living there. It was an enormous upheaval, in many ways, to leave my settled life in the UK, but I just knew I had to go. I was completely true to my Self... and was fortunate (or had had enough experiences?) to know what my real Self was.

I had always been opportunistic. It's no good saying, "If it's meant to happen then it will." Maybe it will. But maybe we also have to play a part in *making* something happen. An internal locus of control is justifiable, just as is an external. For me the key is to listen to the world around. The messages are there: there is no need to scrabble under metaphorical stones or lift up metaphorical bits of rotten wood... just try to tune in to what is around. By tuning in we are becoming in harmony with the Whole. With purity of intention, some protection, discipline and an open heart, we can all find our way.

I do not like the word 'supernatural'. It implies things beyond Nature. 'Esoteric' is fine, because it means 'hidden'.

None of what I've described here has been supernatural. It is all perfectly natural. It may be esoteric, but I am nothing special. However, the world of Nature is quite extraordinary... it is, actually, rather 'super'!

BOOKS

O is a symbol of the world, of oneness and unity. In different cultures it also means the "eye," symbolizing knowledge and insight. We aim to publish books that are accessible, constructive and that challenge accepted opinion, both that of academia and the "moral majority."

Our books are available in all good English language bookstores worldwide. If you don't see the book on the shelves ask the bookstore to order it for you, quoting the ISBN number and title. Alternatively you can order online (all major online retail sites carry our titles) or contact the distributor in the relevant country, listed on the copyright page.

See our website **www.o-books.net** for a full list of over 500 titles, growing by 100 a year.

And tune in to myspiritradio.com for our book review radio show, hosted by June-Elleni Laine, where you can listen to the authors discussing their books.

MySpiritRadio